MW01382169

# DUSTY PLAINS & WARTIME PLANES

# DUSTY PLAINS & WARTIME PLANES

JOHN WAIT, JR.
& JOHN S. WAIT

BLKDOG

www.blkdogpublishing.com

## Other titles by John Wait

*Mortal Musings: Waiting for Dawn*

# DEDICATION

Most importantly, this book is dedicated to my late father, John Wait, Jr. whose life story this book is about. Without him, not only would this book not be here, I would not be here. His story continues to be an inspiration to myself and my family.

It is also dedicated to my mother, who meant so much to my father – as well as to all of us. It was always clear to us kids how much our parents cared for us. They gave us a great environment that helped shape us all to be happy and successful. And to my two sisters, Cheryl and Juliette, who provided information for the books and who shared my love of my father and his story.

Also included are my wife, Holly and two kids, Elizabeth and Matthew, who have provided me endless love and support. Without Elizabeth, it is unlikely this book would ever have been written as she unintentionally inspired Dad to write his story, which none of us really knew or understood.

Not to be left out is my father's extended family... especially his remaining brother, Merle, and sister, Doris, who shared many of his early experiences. My Kansas family has always been very close to my heart. I spent several summers with them, and those experiences shaped who I am today.

But most of all, this book is dedicated to all the members of the greatest generation, whose sacrifices and perseverance are responsible for so much of what we have today. May we always remember them in our hearts and minds.

# FOREWORD

This is the story of my father, John Wait, Jr. I believe it demonstrates why many have called people of his generation, "The Greatest Generation."

The book paints the picture of two epic eras in our history – the Great Dust Bowl (which coincided with the Great Depression) and World War II – through a Midwesterner's eyes. His stories provide vivid images of growing up in dire poverty, yet achieving his ambition of being a pilot, only to have it taken away – then given back, then taken away again.

When we were growing up, my father rarely spoke of his actions during the war – or the difficulties he faced growing up. What finally triggered his willingness to share his story came from an unlikely source – my daughter – then eight years old. They were studying World War II in her third-grade class and she emailed my father to ask what he did. His response surprised us all, as he gave a fairly detailed two-page letter response. It was the first time any of us kids could remember him talking about the war in such detail. He followed the letter with more letters, each growing in detail. Finally, I convinced him to write down his whole story for everyone to read. What follows is that story – much from his own pen, supplemented with details I got from questioning and interviewing him.

Only a few names in this book have been changed, some to protect them as they are not-so-kindly portrayed in the book, and others simply because of gaps in fifty plus year memories. We have gone to painstaking lengths to be as accurate as possible regarding dates and events, even though some apparently conflict with some of the histories we have read.

This book was originally self-published as a Christmas present for my father nearly twenty years ago. I had twenty-five copies printed, which my father gave out to family and his closest friends. There was no real talk about publishing the book, and back then there were no e-publishing companies that make publishing so much easier today.

Sadly, my father passed in July 2016. I regret deeply he was not around to see his book published for mass-distribution. But I know he would have loved it.

We miss you dearly, dad. But it gives us great pleasure to see at least part of your life preserved and shared so others may also benefit from knowing at least part of you.

John S. Wait III

# PROLOGUE

I never imagined one day writing a book about my life. Of course, it has taken me eighty-two years to finally consent to put my life's story – at least the early years – in print. It came about innocently enough when three years ago, my then eight-year-old granddaughter Elizabeth[1] e-mailed me asking what I did during World War II. It seems her third-grade class was studying the war and the fact she had a grandfather who had actually been there was considered pretty "neat".

Not wanting to disappoint her, I fired back an email about two pages in length, attempting to explain some of the things I did. Well, after I sent it off, I realized I left off some rather important information (at least to me). So, I revised my letter, doubling it in size, and sent it. I really hadn't thought much of my experiences in the war before her request – leaving it in the past as I am prone to do with most things that have occurred in my life. I prefer

---

[1] Editors Note: This was written in 1992. Elizabeth is now 28.

to dwell in the present, not the past.

Prior to Elizabeth's inquiry, I hadn't discussed with my family my war experiences, except to give them very cursory details. I just didn't like to talk about it. But I guess as I have grown older and found the past slipping by me at too rapid a rate, I find those memories I have left are more precious. I also feel a greater obligation to pass them on to the present generations – lest they forget what my generation went through to provide them the luxuries, lifestyles and liberties they often take for granted.

So, after sending the revised letter to Elizabeth, I continued to reflect on my war days. I realized I had left more and more out of my brief synopsis. Thus, I revised my letter again . . . and again . . . and again. Over the next few weeks, I found my simple synopsis had grown to more than five single-spaced typed pages. Even then, I knew all I was providing was a cold description of only the substantial facts of those incredible years that meant so much to me.

The five-page letter certainly had a remarkable effect . . . though not necessarily on Elizabeth. Her class had long since moved on to other topics. However, I found my letter made the rounds (thanks to my son) to all my kids and grandkids -- all of whom clamored for more and more details. Finally, that winter (when the weather became inhospitable for golf), and with my son's strong encouragement, I decided to start writing in greater detail about my war experiences.

As I started getting into it, my family (mostly my son) also badgered me to write about my earlier experiences – of growing up in rural Kansas during the Dust Bowl and Great Depression, which overlapped. I realized these experiences were important to share, not only because they reflect an important part of our country's history (as well as my own), but because events that occurred during those times helped shape the me that entered the war.

I am proud of my accomplishments during the war, although I realize I'm not one of the "heroes" por-

trayed in the movies (ever notice how many of them died
to become a hero?) But I think what I did while over there
was important and, at least in a small way, helped us win
the war.

I also managed to bring back a few mementos
from my World War II days. One, a box of German medals I was able to acquire by being one of the first
Americans in Hitler's bunker following his suicide. But by
far, the most important thing I brought back from the war,
even more important than my memories and experiences,
was my wife.

When talking to Americans about World War II,
two events usually stand out – the attack on Pearl Harbor
that hurled us into war – and D-Day, which went a long
way to helping end it – at least in Europe. I was in training
when the attack on Pearl Harbor occurred and will talk
about my reaction to it a bit later. However, I was in the
European Theater on D-Day. And I definitely had a
unique vantage point for the aerial component of the attack. Indeed, I was almost responsible for taking out the
lead plane in the invasion! Let me explain.

When I was sent to Europe in the summer of
1942, I was a fighter pilot and a damned good one too. (All
fighter pilots need to be cocky to a degree – if they hope to
survive. But I honestly feel I could fly with the best of
them.) I was with the 52nd Fighter Group stationed initially out of Londonderry, Ireland. We were sent there, we
believed, to knock the Nazis out of the sky. That was what
we were trained for, that is what we lived for. But fate had
other things in store for me.

So, when June 6th, 1944 came around, I was
mostly flying a desk. I was a First Lieutenant in the Air
Force (or back then, the Army Air Force) and assigned to
the newly formed Headquarters and Headquarters Squadron (yes, that was its real name) for the just as newly
formed 302nd Transport Wing. My job title was "Flying
Control Officer" and I was stationed at Heathrow (yes,

that Heathrow) Air Base in London. Essentially, I ran the air base. I was responsible for every plane – in the air or on the ground – while they were at Heathrow. The control tower was under my supervision.

While my duties kept me grounded, I was still a pilot. As such, I was entitled to extra flight pay (which was significant), as long as I flew at least four hours a month. And one of the nice side benefits to being the Flying Control Officer at Heathrow, was it made it quite convenient to get in my required flying time. One of the days I picked to do so happened to be Tuesday, June 6th, 1944.

June 6th was a beautiful day for flying with clear skies and a warm, gentle breeze. I checked out my favorite Tiger Moth and took off. The British Tiger Moth is a biplane, similar to the American Stearman, but more powerful. It was fun to fly and great for doing aerial acrobatics – which I loved to perform.

I thought I had the entire sky all to myself. I had not seen another aircraft all day. I was doing my usual aerobatic stunts when I decided to do a big loop-de-loop. The initial part of the loop was great, but then as I was coming out of the loop, and going horizontal again I suddenly found myself staring into the eyes of a pilot flying a C-47 pulling a glider behind it. And I was heading right for him.

In a fraction of a second, I realized not only was I not alone, but the sky was literally crowded with planes, all traveling in the same direction -- southward towards France. It reminded me of a football kick-off, except the scope was enormously greater. In a straight line, all the way to the horizon to the left were planes. And as far as I could see to the right, there were more. Thousands of them. They were stacked in layers, too. C-47's pulling gliders[2] at the lowest level. Above them were more C-47s (with paratroopers on board), and above them bombers, and above them fighters. Probably no other human being has ever been privileged to witness the amazing sight I was seeing, at least from the vantage point I saw it – which was a little too close for comfort!

Instantly, I knew what was going on, and I also knew in that fraction of a second that if I didn't do something damn quick, I was going to take the lead plane out of action, myself with it. A C-47, in the best of circumstances, is not a highly maneuverable aircraft. One pulling a glider, like the one in front of me, was virtually helpless.

In less time than it's taken to write this sentence, I hit the joystick hard and dived, nose first, straight down. I leveled off at treetop height and just marveled at the sight passing by above me. Thousands of planes! And they just kept coming. It was truly an awesome sight.

What I didn't know then was that in about three weeks' time, I would be going in the same direction these planes were traveling. But I would be doing my work on the ground, performing essentially the same work as I was at Heathrow.

OK, I guess I shouldn't start a story in the middle. Let's journey back to the start.

---

[2] These gliders were filled with soldiers. I believe about fifteen or so per glider. The gliders would land inland so they would get behind German lines. The C-47s had additional paratroopers on board who would jump behind enemy lines to take out a specific target.

# GROWING UP

I guess the best place to start is at the beginning – well my beginning anyway. I was born on March 22, 1920 in a small unpainted wooden house on the plains. It was a couple of miles from the nearest town, Protection, Kansas, which had a population of about 800 people then (it's much smaller now). Protection was a small farming community located in Comanche County in western Kansas, a few miles from the Oklahoma border. The nearest city was Dodge City, Kansas about fifty miles away. The nearest good-sized city was Wichita, some 150 miles distant.

Mom gave birth to me in our house. No doctor was present. The nearest hospital was in Dodge City, too far to go when you only had horses for transportation, which is all my family had at the time. So, in those days you took things into your own hands. That may be part of the reason there was such a high infant mortality rate. Sadly, I had two siblings die before they were two -- one was the twin of my youngest sister, Doris.

My parents were John and Minnie Wait. I was John Junior but always called "Junior" by family and friends. Like my father before me, I have no middle name, which caused me no end of grief when I was in the military. Apparently, the military just is not set up to accept individuals without middle names. As a result, they gave me all sorts of middle initials throughout my career, although the most frequent was "N.M.I." -- "No Middle Initial." (Ironically, my wife, Shirley Selby, also lacked a middle name before we married, then she used her maiden name.)

I was the middle of five surviving children. I have two older sisters, Ruth and Maxine, a younger sister, Doris and a younger brother, Merle.[3]

My siblings and I were born and raised in a three-room house on our rented 160-acre farm. Our house had a kitchen, a single bedroom (where my parents and babies would sleep) and a family room. That's it. Us kids slept on the bare floor in the family room. There was no plumbing nor bathrooms in the house, not even an outhouse outside. We could not afford one. Just an eight-acre grove of trees we used for privacy when the need arose, and weather permitted.

I'm not going to recount all the details of my childhood. For one thing, it's been a long time and I simply don't remember a lot of them. For another, I'm sure it would be boring to most readers. However, I will mention a few stories to give the you a feel for what it was like growing up in rural Kansas during the "Roaring Twenties" and later during the "Great Depression" and, in particular, the "Dust Bowl" years.

It may come as a shock just how much things have changed. I'm sure you know we didn't have things like computers, video games or even television in those days.

---

[3] Editor's note: As of this writing, only the younger siblings remain.

But you may not have realized just how many of the things we take for granted today were luxuries in those days – luxuries we didn't have. For example, we had neither electricity nor indoor plumbing. Since the grove of trees behind the house we used for a bathroom was not always convenient, we used what was called a "slop" jar,[4] which was kept in the house, especially when the weather was really cold.

My family didn't get electricity or indoor plumbing until after I left for the war. We did not have a car until 1925 (when I was five), relying solely on horses to get around. Dad's first car was an Essex. And it wasn't much of a car. It was so under-powered Dad had to shift into low gear for the smallest hill. We still needed to use the horses to take heavy loads into town.

We took our baths in a washtub in the kitchen. We heated the water on the wood stove. Of course, having no plumbing, we had to bring the water in from the well. Fortunately, it was not too far from the house, about fifteen feet from the kitchen door. Water was lifted from underground by pumping vigorously on the pump handle . . . and pumping . . . and pumping. We took the water inside using buckets – or whatever was handy.

Even though we were dirt poor, we didn't know it. Everyone else around us was also poor. But we had each other. And my father was a very hard worker and would later make a success of himself. He left school in the eighth grade to start working. In fact, neither of my parents had an education beyond eighth grade – yet all five of their children went to college. That was really a remarkable accomplishment for a rural Kansas family in the 1940's. (We

---

[4] A slop jar is more like a pail with a lid.

actually aren't sure how far my dad went through school. My sisters Doris and Maxine say Dad went through eighth grade, but I don't think he went that far. Both based their opinion on the fact Maxine has a picture of Dad in a basketball uniform. I know Dad played basketball, but I remember Dad saying it was a City team he played on. It had nothing to do with the school. In any case, they never played league basketball in grade school in those days. In fact, they still don't as far as I know. We certainly didn't when I was in school.)

*Fun Fact: My brother, Merle, still has the house where I was born. He moved it to his farm, where it is now a storage shed. The house is pictured above. Back then, though, there were no metal walls or roof. And it now has electricity! A luxury we did not have back then. Still no plumbing, though.*

Actually, even going through eighth grade was quite an accomplishment in those days. Yet, although my father wasn't very educated (at least by today's standards), he certainly valued education. In fact, his older brother, Ray, through scholarships and working as a teacher, was able to go onto college and then on to earn his PhD from Iowa State. He later became famous as one of the world's foremost authorities on ions. Indeed, he was involved in the

"Manhattan Project" – the American development of the Atomic bomb. We believe it was his prolonged exposure to radiation from witnessing the nuclear blasts that contributed to his early death.

My father also became very well respected within the community, becoming the first farmer in the County to grow alfalfa and was well known for his excellent crops. He even served as County Commissioner from 1936-1940. But that was later. In the early days, we didn't even own the land we lived on, as Dad rented the farm.

*Our new home (1930)*

When I was about ten years old (1930), we moved into a much bigger house on a farm about 1-¼ miles further west and that much closer to town. It was a two-story house with five bedrooms. Finally, we got a measure of privacy. Later, it even got that most cherished of luxuries – an outhouse! (The outhouse was courtesy of FDR – President Roosevelt. It was not a highly published program, but the federal government built our outhouse because we couldn't afford to build one ourselves.) But we still had no electricity or indoor plumbing. With seven people and five bedrooms, there was some sharing of rooms, but a lot better than before. We also managed to make room for my mother's parents, Grandpa and Grandma Sinkle, when Grandma became ill. Unfortunately, she died shortly after moving in with us. Grandpa Sinkle, however, managed to live to be 99, dying two months shy of turning 100! He stayed with my parents until his death.

\* \* \*

One story about those times I can relate. I remember a fierce blizzard in March 1927. I believe that was the year, because I think I was in first grade at the time. The blizzard struck suddenly and dramatically.

My older sisters and I were on a school bus when it hit. (Yes, we had school buses back then). The school bus got stuck and my sisters and I, along with about a dozen other kids, had to stay at a neighbor's home about one mile from our house. The blizzard did not let up, and we ended up staying with them for a whole week. (Can you imagine having all those kids staying with you unexpectedly?) Nothing moved. Meanwhile, at my folk's house, the same thing happened. Another school bus got stuck near my folk's house. When he saw what happened, my dad hitched up his faithful team, Prince and Queen, to the wagon and brought the sixteen kids who were stranded on the other bus back to the house. The kids spent several nights there. The storm completely shut down the entire area.

I really can't remember much about my stay with the other family, except that it was very crowded. One memory does remain, however. They didn't have plumbing or an outhouse either. That meant a communal slop jar was used – to everyone's unpleasant dismay (no bathrooms, remember).

The main worry for my folks was whether there would be enough food for everyone. Fortunately, there was, but not by much. When the storm abated after a few days, dad hitched a team of horses to a wagon and cut across fields to bring us home.

Of course, in those days, the houses were not very well insulated – just what the wood from the outside walls provided – which was not much. Nor did we have storm windows. For warmth, we huddled around the wood stove, which threw off an amazing amount of heat. In fact, when we had it fully loaded, the whole stove glowed red. Of course, the stove had to be kept fed, which meant a lot of firewood chopping. We joked that the firewood provided two heats – one from the fire and one from all the sawing, chopping and splitting.

Living on a farm meant there was always a lot of work to be done. And I would spend a lot of time doing it. There was little time for fun and games – but we managed.

In those days working the farm was a lot different than farming today. For one thing, we didn't have tractors – at least not until I was eight. We used horses to pull the plows and other farm implements. Much of the very labor-intensive work, like harvesting, would be done communally, with several neighbors getting together to do one person's farm. When that one was done, they would move on to the next. We relied a lot more on our neighbors back then . . . We had too. It certainly helped promote a much stronger sense of community than one normally finds today. The amount of labor required to run a farm was probably also responsible for there being more large families in those days as well. You couldn't afford to hire labor, so you grew your own.

My morning routine consisted of first going into the pasture with my trusted dog, Tippy, who was great working with animals. Usually we had to bring in a herd of about ten-twelve milk cows plus the workhorses if they were scheduled to be used that day. I also helped milk the cows and crank the cream separator. Because there was no electricity, everything was done manually.

We kept pigs, horses, cows, and chickens in addition to farming. The chickens, pigs and some of the cattle were used to feed us. We also produced some milk for sale.

The whole milk was packaged in five-gallon cans. A commercial truck came by each morning to pick up the full cans and left us some clean empties. The milk money provided needed supplementary income since wheat crops were never guaranteed and the price for wheat was never very good during the '30s. Meanwhile, the skim milk that came from what we ran through the separator was fed to the pigs and chickens. My mother used the cream coming from the separator in her cooking and to churn into butter, once it became sour.

Preserving meat was a problem, since we had no refrigeration. One method was to smoke it. Several farmhouses, including ours, had a small, tightly enclosed building used for smoking meat. Another method was to coat the meat in a heavy layer of salt. Since both methods adversely affected the meat's taste, they were used sparingly, or when preferable methods were not available. Such an alternative was neighborhood sharing. In our neighborhood, there were about half a dozen farmers who took turns butchering (we butchered our own meat, which is why I've always had my steaks cooked well-done). Each farmer shared in taking home different parts of the animal. In this way, the quantities taken weren't large enough for the meat to spoil before being cooked and eaten. Of course, households were fairly large in those days, with lots of mouths to feed. Food seldom lasted long enough to spoil.

We were pretty self-sufficient on the farm. In addition to raising our own livestock, mom had her chickens, which furnished us with meat and eggs, and she also maintained a vegetable garden. About the only things we purchased from the local grocery store were flour, salt, sugar, canned goods, and miscellaneous items such as yeast for making bread, and oatmeal for breakfast, etc.

Wheat was our main crop, and because of Kansas' semi-arid climate and soil conditions, it probably always will be. It consistently produces better than any other agricultural plant. As a secondary crop, we grew milo and corn as cash grain crops, but because Dad and many other farmers dabbled in fattening cattle, we also grew sorghum and alfalfa to supply winter feed for the cattle and horses when the pasture grass was dormant.

# ENTERTAINMENT

For entertainment, we often went into town. There was a movie theater we went to. Of course, when I was little, we didn't have "talkies" – the movies were silent. Instead, there would be a piano player in the theater who would play along with the movie. The movies cost a dime. One movie in particular I remember was a silent movie about WW1. (Of course, back then we did not call it "World War I," It was either "The War" or "The War to End all Wars." We never imagined we would be doing the same thing a few decades later.) What really got my attention were scenes showing WW I planes doing aerial dogfights – plane-to-plane-combat. It was this movie that first got me interested in flying. It just looked like a lot of fun! Maybe it was the idea of being in all the open space, coming from a small three-room house shared by seven people!

My father liked going to area rodeos, when he would allow himself the time for relaxing. I remember going to one and watching the clowns riding on top of barrels. They would turn these big 55-gallon barrels on their side, then climb on top and start walking and moving the barrel along as they walked on top.

Well, I thought that was pretty neat. So, I went home and decided to try it with my good friend Webb. I did pretty well, too . . . until I came to a downhill slope.

We also tried other stunts. On one, I was on my horse Baldy and Webb was in a cart I pulled along with a lariat rope. Baldy somehow got tangled up in the rope. He got spooked and reared up, snapping the rope that had been wrapped around the saddle horn. As a result, the rope hit my little finger, breaking it. I was thrown from Baldy and Webb got tossed from the wagon. Baldy raced home, still pulling the wagon. When my mom saw Baldy return, she knew something was wrong and we were stranded. She came and found us. My little finger is still crooked. Thus, my rodeo clown career ended at the tender age of ten.

We got our first radio around 1930. You may be surprised to learn it was a very big deal back then. Since we didn't have electricity in the house, our radio ran on batteries. The family gathered around the radio in the evening and listened – much like families later gathered around the television.

As a teenager for fun we often went into town to "drag" main – which meant simply driving up and down Main Street, waving at everyone we passed. When we got too bored, we simply went to the next town. (I understand this tradition is still common in a lot of small towns in Kansas and elsewhere).

Another vivid memory from my childhood was the rabbit drives. Rabbits were an enemy to the farmers because they ate the crops – affecting the livelihood of virtually everyone in the area. And the rabbits, being rabbits, got awfully thick, destroying crops in the process.

To combat this threat, from time to time we had rabbit drives. These were so important, they let out high school so the boys could help. We didn't use guns for these drives. We used clubs. We would take a square mile section (640 acres). In the middle, they erected a snow fence pen, with just one opening. When they let out school, they dropped us off on the perimeter of the field, stationed about 100 yards apart, all around the square. They picked a time, say 1 pm, (like a shotgun start at a golf tournament), then we started walking. Everyone started heading towards the center, pounding the ground with our clubs. The rabbits got frightened and moved towards the pen. We literally drove thousands of rabbits into the pen. A commercial outfit came and bought the rabbits and sold their hides on the market. The rabbit meat was canned as pet food.

Mom and Dad around 1934

We also hunted rabbits with our .22 rifles. This was as much a chore as sport since the rabbits were such a nuisance.

Another thing we did for entertainment was swimming. There were two swimming pools in the area – one in Protection and one in neighboring Coldwater. During the summer, we went whenever we had the free time.

There was one other swimming spot in the area, although not a pool. I remember us taking a trip to Wilmore, which was also located in Comanche County,

northeast of Protection and Coldwater. Some fellow had
built a pond. On the pond he constructed a huge slide. His
pond and slide became the main recreational spot for the
area.

On this particular day, we went there to listen to a
speech being given by a man running for Governor. His
name was Dr. Brinkley. Well, my parents were going
there to listen, I was going there to have fun on the slide.

Dr. Brinkley had a theory he was peddling, both
commercially and politically. It involved using goat glands
as a treatment for cancer. Most of us – even the farmers --
knew he was a quack. But we enjoyed listening to him, as
he was a gifted and entertaining speaker. Dr. Brinkley put
on a radio show out of Del Rio, Texas that was aimed for
the Kansas market. For the show, he hired a western style
band that played good music. Then he did some political
talking. And people listened.

The pond, or small lake, or however you would
describe it, had become quite a recreational center. The
huge slide ran from up on a hill down to the pond. He installed a pump that brought water to the top of the slide,
where it would then make its way down the slide to the
pond. The slide had a steel bottom to it. To ride, you used
a surf-type board you could rent from him – or make your
own. A lot of folks made their own. The boards looked like
Toboggans. Two or three people could ride in a toboggan
at once. And it was a long slide, on a steep hill. As a result,
you picked up a lot of speed going down.

I can remember riding down the slide with dad
and thinking it was a terrific thrill. The slide flared out at
the bottom and you just kind of shot out of it. You could
go sailing a long way across the lake -- clear across the
pond in fact, because of the great speed you built up going
down that ramp.

So, if you thought all these water amusement parks
were a new invention, now you know we had one out in
the middle of Western Kansas back in the 1920's! It might

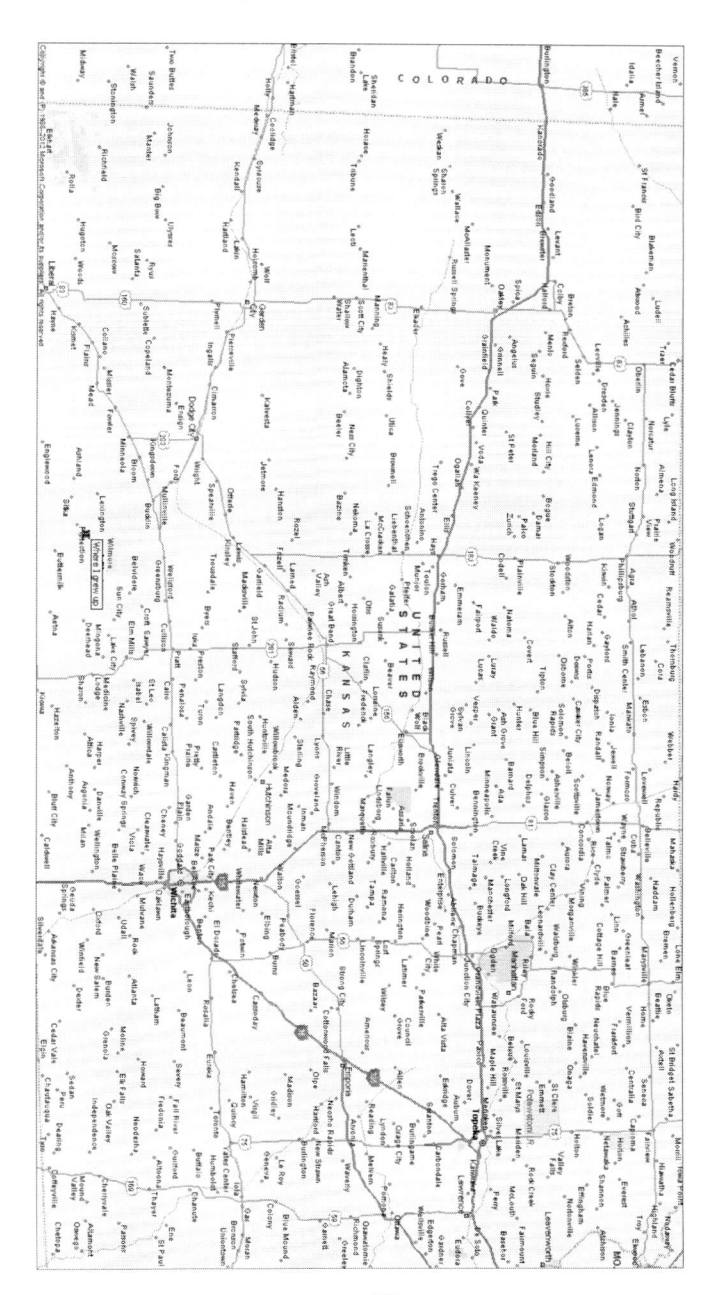

23

not have been as fancy as today's parks – but I bet it was just as much fun.

I can also remember going to a filling station in Protection where the guy made his own toboggan. People liked his so much, he went into business making them for other people. He sold a lot.

I don't remember what happened to that place. I don't think Dad went back – he was so busy. And of course, if he didn't go, we couldn't go.

Back to Brinkley. There was a big crowd there that day listening to Dr. Brinkley. I wasn't much interested in hearing him speak, gifted though he may be. I was much more interested in playing on the slide! I think my parents listened because he was a great talker. But they were not taken in by his "spell." Not many people were. At least, he didn't get enough votes to get elected.

I believe that was the same year as the grasshopper invasion – around 1926. The grasshopper invasion was reminiscent of bible stories of the plagues foretold by Moses in his attempt to free his people. Instead of locusts, we had grasshoppers.

I remember we were still at the place where I was born. The grasshoppers ate anything green and growing – and some things that weren't, such as the bark off of wood fence posts. Of course, we always had plenty of grasshoppers during harvest time. But it was never anywhere near as severe as it was during this particular invasion. And, as far as I know, the invasion was localized to our valley.

The attack occurred during very hot weather, around the harvest in late June or July. They came in such massive numbers; it is hard to describe – or believe. They were so hungry and numerous, they not only ate all of our crops, they ate the weeds as well. They completely stripped the trees of all the leaves, leaving them to stand naked as though it was mid-winter. It was surreal. Sadly, several of the older trees died. But once the grasshoppers finally left or died off after a couple of weeks, the younger trees sprouted new leaves and continued to grow.

The grasshoppers were so thick on the roads, you could look back and see the car tracks from all the 'hoppers that had been crushed. On the shady side of the fence posts and trees, the 'hoppers were several layers thick. On the sunny side, there might none, or just a few. They also appreciated the relief from the summer heat.

No one has ever been able to explain this invasion to me. It just happened. They came, they ate, they destroyed, they left.

As often is the case, this oddity begat another. A natural enemy of the grasshopper is the seagull. And sure enough, there in Western Kansas, in the very middle of our country and about 1,000 miles from any shore, we had hundreds of seagulls feasting like never before. Although you normally wouldn't associate seagulls with the state located in the exact center of the 48 contiguous states, we frequently saw them in the summer. They always followed the plows, which brought up insects as they turned the soil. Farmers do not use plows much these days, now doing "no-till" farming to conserve the soil, so that might cut into the seagulls' incentive to make the trip to the middle of the country.

But in this case, I don't think the seagulls or any other birds, ate enough grasshoppers to significantly lessen the supply. In fact, the grasshoppers were so thick and plentiful and hungry, they chewed on the birds!

I think the grasshoppers just died their natural death. Fortunately, they never returned in those numbers again. We still have grasshoppers, of course, big ones, that come every summer around harvest time. But their numbers are modest enough that they pose no serious problem. The birds seem to keep them in check.

# DUST BOWL

I n Kansas, the "Roaring Twenties" were followed by the "Dirty Thirties," which was meant literally It was during this time we became the "Great Dust Bowl"[5] due to drought conditions and blowing winds that created mammoth dust storms. These dust storms were not only very dirty – but they would completely destroy fields and crops. They were good only for the soap industry! As the entire country was already in the midst of the Great De-

---

[5] The great Dust Bowl, topic of John Steinbeck's 1939 novel, *The Grapes of Wrath*, impacted 100 million acres spread over several states – including Kansas, Oklahoma, Texas, Colorado and New Mexico. It was so called because of the massive dust storms that occurred during this period. These storms often reduced visibility to a few feet. It started in the early 1930s following several years of sustained draught. But poor farming practices also was a major contributing factor. During the draught, strong winds picked up dirt and other loose materials and blow them as a great dark cloud often long distances – even as far as the Atlantic coast. It destroyed crops and farms and forced thousands of people to flee west. The dust bowl lasted several years and spread to several other states. It didn't end until .940. It permanently changed farming practices from that point on.

pression, the Dust Bowl for the Midwestern farmers was like getting kicked in the groin while you were already on the ground reeling from a blow to the head.

The dust bowl affected us far more than the Great Depression – We were already very poor, so the Depression did not really make that much of a difference as we didn't have enough money to own any stock (other than livestock). The banks going broke and unemployment jumping to 25% affected us some, of course. However, the big blow was when the price of wheat dropped to twenty-five cents a bushel. That was below the cost of production!

The Dust Bowl and the Depression coincided, but that was more serendipity rather than being related. Although I'm sure the Dust Bowl didn't help matters much. It lasted several years – I think from around 1933 to just before the war – 1939 or 1940. The dust storms were always in the winter and early spring months, when the wheat cover was minimal, or in real dry years, non-existent. It was also the windy part of the year in Western Kansas. We never had dust storms in the hot summer or early fall months.

The storms varied in both intensity and style. For example, there was the kind where a person could be standing on his front porch on a very windy day, and there's no dust where he's standing. However, he can see dust blowing off the tops of sandy hills in the fields ahead and in the distance. Then there is the type when a dark cloud, like a thick fog, rolls in on a perfectly clear day. And it quickly gets so dark and thick a person literally can't see his hand in front of his face. To give you a better idea, I will describe one such particular dust storm. This is the type of storm Western Kansas became famous for during the "Dirty Thirties." This storm was so dramatic, it left a lasting impression on me. I still remember it clearly to this day.

It occurred sometime during March 1935, or near the time of my 15th birthday, which is how I remember the date. Lawrence Rich, a friend and neighbor, and I rode across his father's wheat field in his father's new rubber-tired John Deere, Model "D" tractor. That places the year because I can remember the Rich's were the first in the neighborhood to get a tractor with rubber tires. In Comanche County, 1934 was the first year for rubber-tired tractors. Previous to that, all farm tractors, including my Dad's, had steel wheels equipped with 5" long steel lugs. The steel wheel models were very rough riding in comparison, and dirty. They were cheaper but less efficient.

Understandably, the Rich's were very proud of their new purchase. I place the month as March, because on the first of April, the young wheat plant is no longer in its dormant winterized stage and driving over it would damage the plants.

I remember we were dressed in shirtsleeves. It was most likely a Sunday, because that was about the only day both Lawrence and I had available to go fishing. Most Saturdays we worked helping our fathers on the farm, and on weekdays, we attended school. Lawrence was two years older than me, but that didn't stop us from fishing together. Our farmhouses were roughly 1/3 of a mile apart.

Our fishing hole was a deep erosion pool carved out by Cavalry Creek. The creek itself ran across the Rich's property and the fishing hole was roughly ½ mile southeast of the house, along the eastern edge of the property. It was about 2 ½ miles due east of Protection.

Let me add just a word about Calvary Creek. I've seen it flood many times. Some of these floods spread out very wide across the relatively flat farmland. But I never saw it run completely dry, even in the hottest, driest years of the "Dirty Thirties." Sometimes, the running stream became fairly small, but you could always see minnows swimming.

It was about 2:30 or 3:00 in the afternoon of a beautiful sunny day, great for fishing or anything else.

Lawrence suddenly jumped to his feet from his spot on the bank, pointed west-northwest, and yelled "Look!"

*This picture was taken in 1934, when I was 14*

Very low in the sky, hugging the ground approximately a mile away, was a grayish-brownish cloud rolling our way. We both knew immediately what it was. We'd seen dust storms before. Hastily, we put our fishing gear away and prepared the John Deere for starting. In those days, farm tractors did not come equipped with batteries or starters. They had to be cranked by hand and with the John Deere, it meant manually rotating a big heavy flywheel. Fortunately, it started. As quickly as we could, we headed northwest towards his parent's farmhouse, and the storm.

Riding on the tractor's fender while Lawrence guided our slow-moving tractor across their wheat field, I had time to both look and ponder. Portions of a science course we had been studying for the past two weeks came to mind. The topic was weather. I loved science. Still do. In our school's weather lessons, we were learning about isobars, millibars, dew points, warm fronts, cold fronts, and occluded fronts. This added a little knowledge and extra interest to what we were witnessing. 'Boy, we should have an interesting discussion tomorrow!' I thought. I'm also thinking I should have a big advantage over at least 95% of my classmates. I'm witnessing the event from open country with an unobstructed view, and it was awesome. All my classmates living in town and even the fellow farm kids who are at home this Sunday won't see the sight we're seeing because of trees and other obstructions. In truth, most won't know until they breathe the dust. Nevertheless, they will have stories to share and someone will undoubtedly have to tell how he, or she, got all chocked up trying to stay alive. Lawrence and I were hoping it wouldn't be us.

Let me try to describe this storm in a way you can get a fairly accurate mental picture of what I witnessed. Start by visualizing a very wide snow avalanche sliding down a steep mountainside. I'm sure you all have seen video of an avalanche. If you haven't, go find one otherwise my description is worthless. Now, mentally turn that avalanche from near vertical to horizontal, slow it down only a tad (it's moving plenty fast) and widen its scope to both horizons, left and right. Except for the color and a few other differences, that's how this approaching dust cloud looked, seemingly chewing up the land as it crawled towards us.

Leading the way for this dirty avalanche was a dusty, tumbling wave. The wave was also visible traveling through a grove of trees surrounding the Rich's house and barnyard. The crest of this advance wave was several feet below the treetops. Surprisingly, to me at least, the concentration, or thickness, of the dust cloud was not evenly spread throughout the wave. It was thinner at the top and thicker or heavier at the bottom. Due north of us was a four-mile open stretch and I could sight along the wave's line and see that it, too, was a little irregular. Trees had slowed its progress in places.

Following the initial wave was a very brief dip or slump. After the dip the cloud sloped upward, but in an undulating fashion and on a near perfect incline looking as though the whole thing continued upward and back indefinitely. Just as the leading wave reached our tractor, I could sight along the dust cloud tops and see the moon in a direct line. At that time, the moon was perhaps somewhere around 1/3 of the way up above the horizon. Assuming it could be made possible to walk across the top of a dust storm cloud, it looked from where I was sitting on the tractor fender as though one could have walked all the way to the moon. The dust cloud looked to stretch that far.

It was at that very split second when I first saw the moon, I realized I had just visually sighted the sloping incline formed by an approaching cold front! Cold air, being heavier than warm air, slides underneath the warmer air. Put another way, from our perspective on the ground, because of that incline or wedge we were actually looking down on the topside of an enormous dust cloud appearing to be endless in size. Incidentally, that topside was also the ceiling of the dust cloud we would very soon be under and inside.

Because of that storm, we had the rare opportunity to have actually seen an incline line separating cold air from warmer air. My regret is that I didn't have a camera to take a color picture of that moon when the front was at our tractor. It would have been a classic! Actually, the moon disappeared rather quickly, mostly from the front's movement.

From http://www.ptsi.net/user/museum/dustbowl.html - Phone appeared in Dodge City Globe. This might be the same storm I saw.

I said color picture for a very good reason. I'm not sure I can adequately describe that particular dust cloud. Notably, its appearance was very different when it was nearby as opposed to distant. When we first spotted it, the dust cloud, looked like a gray-brown (mostly gray) cloud hugging the ground. But the very top of the cloud glistened just as brightly as any water vapor cloud. Remember, it was a cloudless, brilliantly sunny day, with the sun fairly high in the near mid-afternoon sky. When I was sighting along the top of the dust cloud toward the moon, the entire path glistened in the sunshine, just as silvery and brightly as any vapor cloud -- with one big difference. The base of each wave, or mound, had a definite light brown tint to it. It was sort of like looking at a platinum blonde's hair then spotting brown roots. In both cases, the true color showed. However, in only an approaching dust storm case does all of these descriptive words apply: brilliant, colorless and repulsive.

When the front passed, there was a wind shift to the north. But the wind strength was relatively light, definitely not strong enough to kick up any dust locally. Regardless, we were breathing cooler, dirtier air, and we knew from experience, it would get significantly worse. The dirty air made it much tougher to breath. (We often put a cloth, or part of our shirt over our mouths to try and filter out some of the dirt. It did not work well.) It took us no more than five minutes to get to Lawrence's house and it took me perhaps another ten minutes to jog home. It was a dirty trip.

As the front continued advancing, the vertical depth of the dust steadily increased until the tops finally reached several thousand feet. In fact, I recall reading a newspaper account that an airline pilot reported seeing a dust cloud topping 20,000 feet. While I have no way of knowing how high this particular cloud reached, I do know our house continued to get dirtier and darker, and the theory goes the higher the storm's ceiling, the thicker the dust near the bottom and the darker it will become.

In about an hour, as the dust made its way into our home, it got so dark my mother lit a kerosene mantle lamp. (Remember, electricity did not arrive at our house for another ten years, while I was overseas during WW2). Nevertheless, the light from the lamp could be clearly seen only if you were close to it. Beyond a distance of eight feet, only a luminous glow in the dusty fog indicated the direction of a source of light. This particular dust storm was, in my opinion, probably the thickest and dirtiest of all I've seen.

Because of the low wind speed during that storm, very, very little of the dust we were breathing was of local origin. While the wind increased somewhat, it was never strong enough to cause much local blowing, which was typical. The reasons were multiple: 1) we were located in a fairly large valley with an abundance of trees (by Western Kansas standards), which lined two other creeks (Bluff and Kiawa) besides the Cavalry, 2) lots of growth and ground cover, 3) few large open fields, and 4) the soil was of a type that didn't blow easily. Therefore, most of the soil erosion damage occurred at a distance of 60 to 300 miles or more to the west and northwest of us. Their topsoil has an entirely different texture.

Further west in the higher high plains, the topsoil becomes fluffy and powder-like when dry. If the ground is bare and smooth, their light topsoil will become airborne with just a slight breeze.

But have no fear. The dust storms of the "Dirty Thirties" aren't coming back. Our farmers have been taught to manage and cultivate their soil entirely differently now (Courtesy of the Agriculture schools). It's called "No till" farming. In short, it means farmers won't plow or loosen the soil or remove any ground cover. Instead, they drill or plant their new crop in the stubble or remains of the old crop. As long as the topsoil has cover, dust storms will remain a legacy of the old "Dirty Thirty" past. Thank God! Surprisingly, yields haven't suffered, however big bucks are now spent for fertilizer whereas in the "Dirty Thirties" little or none was used or needed.

Also helping substantially reduce the risk of future storms, was a program started by FDR. Later referred to as "Roosevelt's Rows" the program involved giving incentives to farmers to plant rows of trees to help break the wind. As a result, there are now rows of trees across the great plains.

# Ft. Hays

The flying bug bit me when I was about eleven or twelve years old. Our family was living in the rickety five-bedroom farmhouse. That house is no longer standing. Also gone are the grainery, garage, barn,

corral, a windmill, hog house, chicken coop, outhouse, a 40-foot concrete silo and an eight-acre grove of trees that were there when I was growing up. They've all been destroyed or plowed under. A routine looking wheat field stands there now. That's progress and it's been repeated many times over the years in Comanche County. As an example, in 1920, the year of my birth, the total population in Comanche County was over 5,000 people. Forty years later, it was down to 3,400. Eighty years later, in the year 2000, it had dropped to less than 2,000 and its still dropping. (Editor's note: it was 1,790 in 2017).

Back in 1931 or 32, the wheat field across the road, south of our house, looked exactly the same then as it does today. But it was more interesting then. A local aviation enthusiast, Melvin Hart, occasionally landed his WWI-type biplane there. Naturally, we kids went to watch. One day when he was in a generous mood, he offered rides to my two older sisters, Maxine, who was about seventeen at the time, and Ruth, who was about fifteen. Later, as an afterthought (plus Maxine's suggestion), he offered me a ride as well. Predictably, their rides were much longer and exciting looking than mine. My ride was very short, just a quick circle around the field. We probably never went more than 200 feet high, and the entire flight lasted no more than ten minutes, if that. But it was long enough. I was hooked! Even though I was barely big enough to see over the sides of the open cockpit, I saw enough. I knew someday I was going to fly, just like Melvin did.

Three or four years ago, in a nostalgic conversation with Maxine, I asked, "Whatever happened to Melvin Hart?" thinking surely, by now, he's long gone. She surprised me when she answered, "I think he's still alive, and living somewhere in the Lake of the Ozarks region." If he is, he's pushing 100 and I'll bet he would be a wealthy source of stories.

My opportunity to cash in on that latent desire to learn to fly came in my sophomore year in college. Ft. Hays State College offered a government sponsored Civilian Pilot Training course in the fall of 1940.

It may surprise you to know that when I first went to Ft. Hays, it wasn't to get an agriculture degree. In fact, I wanted to study Psychology. In High School, we had learned about Sigmund Freud and I read a book about him and became fascinated. However, when I got to Ft.

Hays, I quickly got disillusioned about making a career out of Psychology.[6]

They had a sanitarium not far from campus. I remember meeting some of the patients there. A few of them were pretty weird. I remember one adult who was terrified of cars. He apparently was told as a youngster to be very careful about crossing the street or he could get run over by a car. So, if he wanted to cross the street, he stood at the curb until there was no car anywhere in sight that was moving. If he saw a car moving, no matter how far away, he did not budge.

But what really put me off Psychology was my first Psychology professor. In Psychology 1, our professor was old and, frankly, a nut. About every other class, he showed up with his fly undone and had to be reminded to zip it up. It annoyed me I was studying from a nutcase. Then I noticed most of the students in the class also seemed to have psychological issues (except me, of course). That did it for me. So, at semester, I changed my major to pre-law. I decided I just didn't want to be associated with all these crazies. Of course, I never became an attorney, either. But that was because I learned to fly.

Another disillusionment I suffered at Ft. Hays was my athletic career. In High School, I played football, which I loved. I started by playing in the backfield. But in my second year, I became an end. Although we played both offense and defense in those days, I specialized in defense. I loved tackling. As a defensive end, I also got to be involved in every play, which I liked. And I thought I was

---

[6] Editor's note: His son (me) did get a Master's degree in Psychology, but left the program A.B.D. (all but dissertation) to start my first business.

pretty good.

When I got to Ft. Hays, I decided to try and further my athletic career by trying out for their football team. It was especially convenient as I was living in the men's dormitory, which happened to be under the football stadium. However, when I tried out for the team, I quickly learned the players playing football in college were a whole lot bigger than those playing for a (very) small town high school. At 5'7 1/2" tall and about 140 pounds, I was not exactly the prototype college football player – especially at end! So, I decided to preserve my body and quit the team.

The reason I picked Ft. Hays in the first place was because it was close and cheap. All my sisters also went to Ft. Hays for the same reasons.[7]

When I got there, I applied for financial assistance. But they didn't have any scholarships available. But they got me a job as a latrine orderly. It may not have been the most pleasant job I could have, but it served its purpose. It helped get me through school.

But I digress. As I mentioned earlier, in my sophomore year I enrolled in Civilian Pilot Training course (CPT). The course consisted of three college-hours academic work on campus (mostly weather and some mechanics) and about thirty-five hours actual flying time at the local municipal airport, or enough for a private pilot's license. It cost me virtually nothing. The exact price I could afford.

I worked very hard on my roommate, Hugh Chance, trying to interest him in taking the course with me. At first, he was very negative and cool to the idea, but

---

[7] Editor's note: His brother was much smarter and went to the University of Kansas (also my alma mater).

at crunch time, he relented and joined me. Turns out, I did him a great favor. I'll tell you why in a bit.

The plane we were to fly and take lessons in was an Aeronca TLD, tandem seating, with a Lycoming 65 HP engine. It had a cruising speed of 85 mph. It was equipped with basic instruments only, no radio. My instructor was Kenneth W. Holmes. We hit it off well right from the start.

Each student was given a logbook (which I still have) where flying time and the instructor's comments were recorded. Below are some excerpts from my logbook, consisting of eight of Instructor Holmes most flattering comments. Naturally, I have no interest in showing you the unflattering comments. Besides, the list is too long and boring.

### Date Day Accum Instructor Holmes Comments
#### Flt Time Flt Time

9-23-40 30 30 Apparently making good start – not outwardly nervous (very first lesson)

9-27 30 2:05 Used some initiative. Fairly quick reactions. Good

10-08 25 6:15 Could have soloed safely

10-11 10 8:00 Made a perfect solo

10-16 40 9:55 Takes to flying like a natural

10-25 45 16:25 Makes the most good landings of any student in the unit.

10-30 50 18:35 Handling a strong wind in a capable manner

12-10 1:05 37:50 Approved for private. Very apt, one of the best in the unit.

Of course, I'm pleased with my instructor's comments, particularly the one with reference to my landing skills. Turned out to be my trademark throughout my flying career in all types of planes. I always made good smooth landings. Well, except for once. I'll tell you about it later.

While the course lasted a total of four months, there really isn't much I could tell you about it. It was all pretty much routine, except for one rather wild flight which I can't resist telling since it included some flying elements I had not been trained for (I found this happening throughout my flying career). Using logic, instinct, and all the flying skill my instructor gave me, the flight ended on a rather exciting, but safe note (or I wouldn't be here to tell the story!).

This particular flight was my very first solo cross-country flight, which, according to my log, was made on December 5, 1940, near the end of the course. Unless you're a pilot, you probably can't fully appreciate the fact that when you first fly solo, you hear rattles, squeaks, and mysterious sounds you've never heard before. You worry, what's going on? What's happening? Of course, I had soloed locally several times, but this was my first trip away from home base all alone, and the journey was to take most of the day.

The day started routinely enough, just a light breeze and beautiful sunshine. My solo journey was to be in two sections, each having a triangle course. The first started from Hays at 8:15 am, going SE 50 miles to Great Bend, where I landed. After the airport manager had signed my course report, I took off on the second leg of the triangle for Russell (where Bob Dole was probably sitting in a senior classroom. Had I known he would be my future Senator, and later Presidential candidate, I would have waggled my wings.)

No landing was required in Russell. It and a couple of other small towns were checkpoints I used before returning to Hays, where I landed at 10:16 am. So far, so good.

John Wait

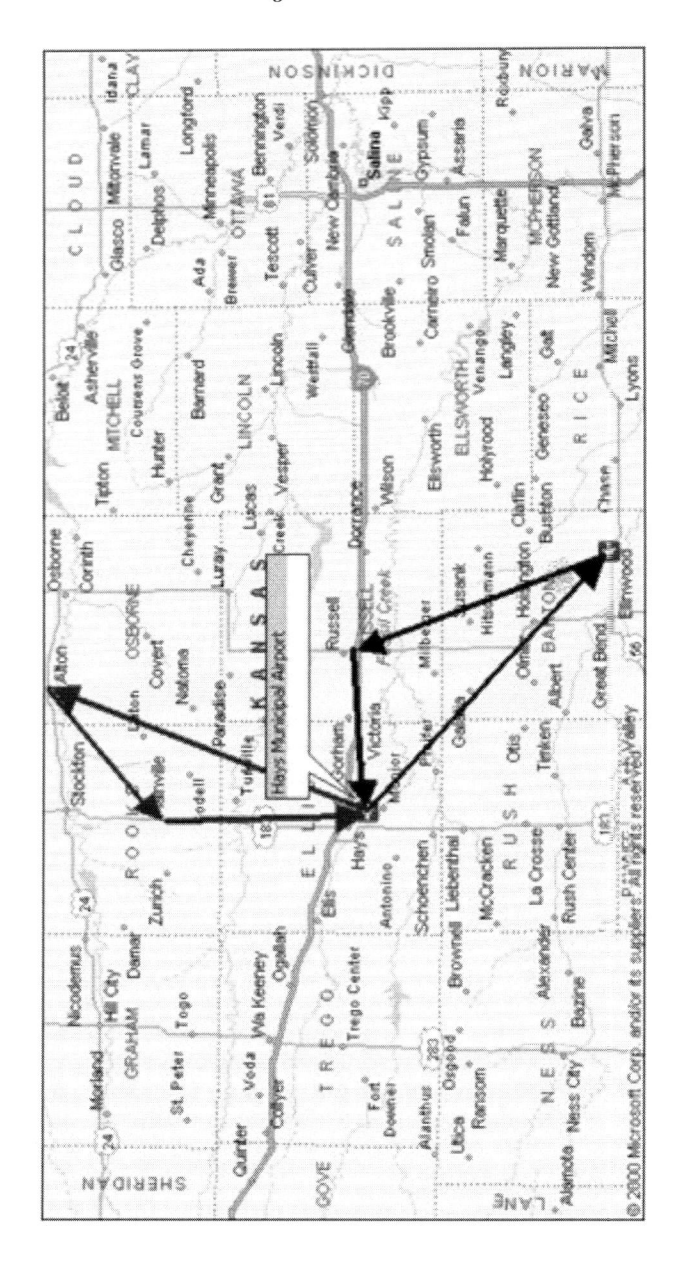

42

After refueling and a hasty snack, I took off at 10:38 to execute the northern triangle of my day's work. The first leg required a landing at Alton, which I did at 11:12. I obtained the airport manager's signature and then took off at 11:30, heading towards Plainville, the second leg. No landing was required there, so my navigation problems over open country were done for the day. I could relax. From Plainville to Hays, all I had to do was fly south, parallel to Highway 281 (now 181), a distance of about twenty-three miles straight into Hays . . . Piece of cake. Nothing to this solo cross-country flying, I thought. The hard part was all done.

I'm cruising along, admiring the scenery, watching a farmer feed his cattle (for a long time) even admiring the speed with which cars and trucks were traveling up highway 281. In fact, it seemed to me they were speeding. Even the trucks were speeding. They were passing me! Then I spotted an old cattle truck, fully loaded with cattle. He couldn't possibly be driving that old relic more than 40 mph, but he passed me like I was standing still. I checked my gauges. The tachometer looked fine, and the air speed indicator said 85 mph, so what's going on here? I looked outside again. Yes, it's boring as the landscape hardly changes. Then I spotted that farmer who was feeding his cattle. I had passed him five minutes ago! Now, I'm backing over him, tail first! That gentle breeze had been replaced by a gale and I was flying right into it.

From both ground school and my flight instructor, I'd learned enough to know that because of surface friction, there is often a considerable difference in the wind velocity at 1,200 feet, where I was flying, then at the surface level. Obviously, the thing to do, if I wanted to get back to Hays, was to 'hit the deck.' So, down, down, down I went, right to fence-post-height where I started dodging tumbleweeds. But my forward progress was now around 25-30 mph (though still not enough to catch that cattle truck).

Fortunately, from this point all the way to Hays, the terrain was entirely grassland. Had there been cultivated fields with blowing dirt, I don't know what would have happened. I definitely would have had to make other plans. As it was, the tumbleweeds were my biggest concern, but over grassland, there weren't many to worry about. To this point, I'd been flying for close to four hours, and normally you'd expect to be getting a little tired, but I wasn't. Now the trip was getting a little interesting, even thrilling.

It was perhaps ten more miles to the Hays airport, which gave me a little time to think about how I was going to safely land this light plane in a near gale force wind. It would take some careful handling. There wouldn't be much room for error, but somehow, I wasn't afraid. It was more of an exciting challenge.

At that time, the Hays airport was an all grass-surface airport. Airport offices and an attached hanger were located somewhere in the SW quadrant. As I approached the airport, there were a few trees requiring me to rise in order to clear. The process of doing that provided a very bumpy ride from the gusty, swirling wind. But maintaining control was really no problem, since I had plenty of airspeed. It was just bumpy. My main interest at that critical point was getting my plane positioned and aligned in such a way that it would be headed both into the wind and directly toward the hanger. The hanger (if my plan worked) was to be my ultimate windbreak.

As I cleared the trees, something else attracted my attention. There was a small mob of people out on the airfield near the hanger. I learned later they were called by the administration to help with my landing. I also learned that when the sudden windstorm hit Hays, they had called the airport at Alton, only to be advised, "too late, he's long gone." And, of course, the plane had no radio.

Though all landings in a gale-force wind entail

some risk, I honestly believe the way I accomplished this one was the simplest and safest way. I literally flew the airplane into the ground, headed directly toward the hanger. Then, when the wheels touched, I slowly reduced the throttle until the ground speed was zero, however, technically, the plane still had flying speed so I didn't dare pull the tail down, or the plane would have taken off, perhaps going backwards! As my plane came to a halt, the mob rushed out, clothes flapping in the breeze, and grabbed my wing tips, wing struts, wheel struts, anything they could hang on to. My instructor made two attempts to open the door to jump in, but the slipstream was too strong, so he backed off and motioned me to taxi forward toward the hanger. I nodded. I knew what he meant. That had been my plan all along.

After the plane was anchored down, I exited the plane to a greeting like a football player gets after scoring a winning touchdown. There was much backslapping, hand shaking and congratulations all around. My instructor even gave me a big hug. Frankly, I felt pretty good about myself.

One final postmortem review of that flight, my final checkpoint between Alton and Hays was Plainville. The official record shows I passed over Plainville at 11:59. Simple calculations show my ground speed from Plainville to Hays was 32 mph. Lance Armstrong rode his bicycle across France faster than that. And for the last ten miles, I was going much slower!

Completion of the CPT course made my next decision easy. I was going to join the Army Air Force. Believe it or not, the war in Europe was not a consideration. I just wanted to fly. At that time, the Air Force required a minimum of two years of college credit before an applicant would be accepted. Consequently, I had another semester to complete. But to expedite matters, I went ahead and took the physical contingent upon my successfully completing my sophomore year. I passed the physical, so all that was left was to finish the second semester.

My ex-roommate and good friend, Hugh Chance, also took the physical. He liked flying so well, he wanted more as well. As fate would have it, it turned out he was colorblind, and the Air Force rejected him. Hugh was crushed. I can vividly recall how dejected he was. He hadn't been aware he was colorblind! It's strange how such little things like being colorblind can have such a tremendous impact on one's life. In his case, it was his fortune. When I returned from overseas and saw him again nearly five years later, he was a senior pilot (Captain) flying for United Airlines out of Denver and earning an incredible amount of money, like $100,000 per year, which in those days, would buy a lot of anything. Somewhat offsetting that was the fact income taxes were much, much higher in those days.[8] I don't think people realize that.

This is how lucky breaks happen sometimes. It seems the Air Force, after Pearl Harbor, called up their reservists, many of whom were airline pilots. This hit the airlines pretty hard. In desperation, United and the other airlines, beat the bushes to find anyone with flying knowledge and experience. When they found Hugh, they grabbed him. They didn't care if he was colorblind. In fact, they liked it. They knew they could count on him not being called up by the military.

---

[8] In 1944, the top tax bracket was 92% of income for those earning over $100,000. It was 84% if you earned over $70,000 per year. It was 50% if you just earned over $14,000.

# TRAINING

On July 16th, 1941, while I was helping Dad finish harvest, I received a Western Union telegram directing me to report to Ft. Riley, Kansas for assignment. This was it! What I'd been anxiously awaiting. I was officially in the Army Air Force.

Since our local train was a spur line terminating at Wichita, Dad drove me to Greensburg, about thirty miles distant, where a train with a direct rail line to Ft. Riley could be caught. As the train approached the station, Dad put his arms around me and started to cry. That was so unexpected, it caught me completely off-guard.

My Dad seldom displayed strong emotion. He had been through a lot of ups and downs, mostly downs, and learned to handle it on a fairly even keel. In all my life up to that point, I'd only ever seen Dad cry one time previously, and that was when I was about nine years old (give or take a year).

In those days, we were poor. That's about the only way to describe it, unless you said very, very poor. We kids didn't know it though. Our neighbors were in similar shape or worse. Dad owned nothing but a saddle horse, two workhorses, two mules, and some horse-drawn farm machinery. Nevertheless, through very hard work, determination, and some resourceful farming methods, he developed a good reputation as a comer. The local banker, having faith in Dad, loaned him enough money to buy a herd of small, young "white faced" calves Dad wanted. Dad expected to make a nice profit feeding the calves from crops he'd raised, and then marketing the calves.

For about six months, he lovingly fed those calves. He fed them just about all the grain and hay we'd raised that year. They looked so good, he speculated he might even get the top price for them when he took them to market. He was right, he did. That was the good news. The bad news was the total selling price did not quite cover the railroad's freight bill to Kansas City. The railroad took the whole check. Dad was left with nothing. He did not even have money to buy return passage home, over 400 miles away.

Out of the goodness of the railroad's "generous" heart, Dad was given passage home in a caboose. If you know anything about cabooses, you know they were extremely austere, dirty and uncomfortable. Seating consisted of a wooden bench with no padding. At each railyard the caboose sustains the same bumping and jostling the freight cars get. In other words, not only was his pockets empty of money, it was a long, torturous two-day ride.

When Dad arrived home, he was, I think, at the lowest point in his life. As he tried to tell us what happened, he broke down and cried. Even though I was pretty young, it was an event that made a big impression on me and I have never forgotten it. As I said, I never saw that kind of emotion from him again until Greensburg, and I was neither expecting nor prepared for it. All I could think to say was, "Don't cry Dad, I'll be coming back, real soon. I'll make lots of visits, you'll see."

What a lousy prophet I turned out to be. My intentions were good, but I had no way of foreseeing the heinous Japanese bombing of Pearl Harbor and the effect it would have. That changed everything. Turned out I saw my Mother and Father at home, in Kansas, only one time between that point (July 1941) and when I returned from overseas in mid-October 1945. The one other time I saw them was when they drove to Phoenix, Arizona, to see me graduate from the military's Luke Field Advanced Flying School (February 6, 1942).

By way of a small postscript, when Dad had his cattle disaster in Kansas City, it was at the point marking the beginning of the Great Depression. What timing. Though discouraged and upset, he did not give up. By working seven days a week (Dad went to church twice a year, all other Sundays were regular work days), from 4 am to long after dark all year round, no vacations, and using his own innovative farming techniques, he managed to raise crops and fatten cattle during the dust bowl and Depression years when farmers all around him were failing. Dad actually made money and greatly increased his own net worth during those horrible years. By 1941, when I went into the service, Dad owned three farm tractors and two wheat-combines. The horses and mules were long gone except for two saddle horses. He also owned 640 acres of farmland and rented over 2,000 more (which was a considerable amount back then), much of which he purchased and paid for during the war years.

* * *

In the summer of 1941 Army Air Force Cadet flight training consisted of three flight training phases: Primary, Basic and Advanced. Each phase lasted 2 ½ months. Actually, it started as three months, but was shortened. In the past, each phase was taught at different airfields, but because the airfield at Cal-Aero was so unusually large, both Primary and Basic were taught there.

There were a number of things I liked about Cal-Aero[9]. In the first place, it was not operated by the mili-

---

[9]In a picture book I have of Cal-Aero, they describe themselves thusly:

"In Southern California, a few miles east of LA, lies a very beautiful fertile valley of green fields, orange groves, and grape vineyards. Here, just south of the city of Orlando, in the shadow of the San Gabriel mountains, is situated CAL-AERO ACADEMY. What today is one of America's largest and finest Civilian Air Corps training centers, was a year ago little more than a wheat field. It is our Cal-Aero that has the distinct honor of having been chosen as the first Civilian Flying School in the history of the U.S. Army Air Corps to teach basic training.

"In the years to come, you will pick up this book, and looking through

tary. It was a civilian base under contract with the government. All instructors were civilian and well qualified. There was a minimum of hazing. What little hazing we experienced was from the student's in Basic training.

Furthermore, Cal-Aero was attractive. It was relatively new with nice living quarters for the cadets and a rather scenic location at the foot of Mt. Baldy in Ontario, California, just outside of Los Angeles. From a functional standpoint, it was vastly superior to ordinary airports for flight training because instead of runways, the landing and take-off area was a vast macadamized[10] expanse. In other words, the entire field, a little less than a square mile is size, was completely paved with asphalt, making it possible to accommodate a lot more take offs and landings than an airport with traditional runways. The fact the prevailing wind was almost always a gentle one from the same direction, made this more plausible.

The plane used for Primary Training was a PT 13B "Stearman" (made in Wichita, Kansas), with a 225

---

these photos, the first important months of training that you spent in the WORLDS FINEST AIR FORCE will be recalled to your memory." They were right.

Encyclopedia Britannica defines macadam construction thusly: "**Macadam**, form of pavement invented by John McAdam of Scotland in the 18th century. McAdam's road cross section was composed of a compacted subgrade of crushed granite or greenstone designed to support the load, covered by a surface of light stone to absorb wear and tear and shed water to the drainage ditches. In modern macadam construction crushed stone or gravel is placed on the compacted base course and bound together with asphalt cement or hot tar. A third layer to fill the interstices is then added and rolled. Cement-sand slurry is sometimes used as the binder."

HP radial engine. It was a biplane, with two open cockpits (much like old WW1 planes). It had basic instrumentation only and no radio. (Just like at Hays). While onboard, the students and instructor communicated with a stethoscope type device. It was necessary for both student and instructor to wear a helmet and goggles, because of the open cockpit. (I have included a picture of me with a helmet and goggles).

Primary training passed without any memorable incidents. I will mention my personal Pilot's Flight Logbook, (which I still have) was maintained by Cal-Aero personnel while I was there. At the end of my Primary course, the accuracy of my flight time (which was 27 hours, 32 minutes dual and 32 hours, 28 minutes solo) was certified by Captain Robert L. Scott, the base commander, on September 30, 1941. That name probably doesn't mean much to you, but besides being the commandant of Cal-Aero, at the time, he happens to be the same fellow who four months after Pearl Harbor, became the famous Col. Robert L. Scott, leader of the Flying Tigers in Burma. They famously flew P-40 fighters, the same fighter I was to fly fresh out of Advanced Flying School. I might also add Robert L. Scott wrote a book that later became a best seller. The title was "*God is My Co-pilot.*"

\* \* \*

For Basic Training we flew a BT 13 Vultee, with a 450 HP Radial engine. It was a sturdy built, low-wing monoplane, with tandem seating and a fighter plane-type sliding canopy. This plane was equipped with a radio and more advanced instrumentation. It did not, however, have retractable landing gear. We got that in the Advanced, or the final stage of training.

Our schedule was quite simple and rigid. We flew, or attended ground school (mostly involving weather, mechanics and navigation) five days a week, Monday through

Friday. Saturday morning was usually military training, marching, etc. Sunday was our day off for church, or an open pass to Los Angeles, or whatever.

On the third Saturday morning after we had finished our marching exercises, we were standing in a very long parade rest formation consisting of both the primary and basic units out on the flight line. We were listening to our base commander, Captain Scott. He gave us some announcements and instructions on how we should cooperate and behave for the Hollywood actors and crew who would soon be coming to our base to make a movie called "Keep 'Em Flying," starring Bud Abbot, Lew Costello and Martha Raye, when out of the west, in direct line with outstanding formation, came this very low flying Stearman. It flipped over in a half roll and flew upside down about 10 feet, directly over our heads with the pilot's white scarf flowing and him waving out of the plane's open cockpit. Then the pilot did another half-roll, turned and landed, just behind us. Talk about a grand entrance! We had just witnessed a very spectacular one, obviously designed to impress a group of student pilots. It did!

\* \* \*

Paul Mantz, a famous stunt pilot, was to do the stunt flying in the forthcoming movie. He was giving us a sample of what we were to witness in the next few weeks, which was plenty. We found out later, the plane he was flying was actually not a Stearman. It was an old Boeing P-12, painted and made over to look like a Stearman. The P-12 had a larger engine, more speed, a higher rate of climb, and increased maneuverability.

Here are some of the stunts we saw over the next several weeks:

- In one scene in the movie, the script called for the plane (shown as being piloted by Lew Costello in the movie) to make a dive at the control tower. Paul Mantz not only came close, he hit it. An antenna connected to the tower balcony was bent at a right angle. I'm sure the fellow sitting in the tower at the time must have climbed down with dirty pants.

- In another scene, a fire truck and an ambulance were supposedly chasing around the field for an impending plane crash when Paul Mantz dived so close to the fire truck, he frightened the driver enough he turned the truck over. The script hadn't called for that action, but since it looked so good, they left it in the movie.

- Paul Mantz also flew straight through four hangers lined up along our flight line, then made a spectacular vertical climb after clearing the fourth hanger. Some of our cadets, who happened to be between the 3rd and 4th hanger, said he was lucky to live through that one. They reported he came dangerously close to hitting the top of the hanger door.

When the movie was finished, the cadets and everyone on base were treated to a large dance on the base, with a big band and live entertainment. It was a gala affair, with all the stars from "Keep 'Em Flying" there as well.

Abbot and Costello even took us on a tour of the studio. We got to talk to them. They were very nice. This was before Pearl Harbor – but not much before – maybe a few weeks. Even then, all the service men were very popular. There was a prevailing opinion we would be getting into the war one way or another. We all knew Hitler had to be stopped. But we didn't give the Japanese a second thought. We had no harsh feelings towards them – until they bombed Pearl Harbor. We didn't even consider them important until then.

One final thing before I leave the movie story. Several other cadets and I were to be in the movie too, in a big way we assumed. We spent hours perfecting our formation drill with cameras rolling and couldn't wait to see ourselves in the movie. Opening night revealed the truth: our big scene in the movie had been cut to, at most, one second. If you blinked, you missed us.

\* \* \*

One Sunday morning a few weeks later, when we were about ¾ through Basic Training, we heard the gut-wrenching news on radio that Pearl Harbor was under attack by a swarm of Japanese airplanes. There were four of us living in our unit, two to a bedroom. We were listening to the news and studying at the time. After the initial announcement all four of us crowded around the radio in shock, listening to the grim details we all knew would greatly affect our lives. Suddenly one of my roommates made a very perceptive announcement. "Hey Fellows! It's Sunday! If we're going to town, we better do it quick. You know they'll close the post."

He was right. The front gate closed immediately after my best friend, Bill McGowan, and I left.

When we checked back around 7:00 PM, we received more bad news. We cadets were going to be taking turns pulling guard duty, guarding our planes. Guess who drew the midnight to 4 AM shift? Yep, I was out there marching around and through our training planes with a gun and live ammunition, watching the stars to see if any were moving and wondering if Japanese paratroopers really were coming. Don't laugh. We weren't. Of course, everybody now knows they weren't coming, but we didn't know it then.

*In the above picture, I am the one Bud Abbot is talking to.*

**Editor's Note**: *The picture above was involved in another interesting story. One of my father's granddaughters, Danielle, opened a bar in Dolan Springs, Arizona. This was about 2008 or so. She had a copy of the picture above and had it framed, then hung it in her bar. One day an elderly patron came up to her and was very angry. He claimed she had no right to hang that picture in her bar. He was demanding she take it down. Confused, she asked why he was so offended. He told her that it was a picture featuring his brother, who had died not long after it was taken. Danielle had to explain to him the reason she had it was that her grandfather was in the picture.*

Pearl Harbor also had the effect of accelerating our training program significantly. Case in point, on Monday, December 8th, the day following the attack on Pearl Harbor, I flew a one-hour dual formation flight training, and over two hours solo formation flight training. The total of three hours and ten minutes was the most time I had spent aloft in one day during my entire Basic Training period.

Remember, this was immediately following having been up half the night doing guard duty. Further, even though Basic Training was originally scheduled to last two more weeks, my last flight in Basic came just two days later on December 10th. Two days after that, I was on my way to Luke Field, in Phoenix, Arizona, for Advanced Flight training.

Looking back on my Primary and Basic training periods at Cal-Aero, I can't recall a single flight I had memorable enough or exciting enough to tell about. In that way, it was unlike my CPT course. Also, unlike my CPT course, I received no written grades, nor written comments from my flight instructors. However, I always had a confident feeling I was doing very well and rightfully I should have done well. Most of the other cadets had never flown before. I always felt the lessons I learned in CPT gave me a big head start over my classmates.

Even though I personally had no exciting flights at Cal-Aero worth recounting, I did happen to observe a very rare and unusual flying incident that happened to a fellow Primary student pilot and it had a significant impact on me.

I was standing between the third and fourth hanger one day, watching the planes take off and land, when suddenly a wheel dropped off a Stearman just taking off. The Stearman was about 70 feet high at the time. A couple of instructors who also witnessed the incident, felt it was important to alert the student pilot to the plight he was in, but were in a quandary as to how to do it since none of the Stearmans were equipped with radios. One of them retrieved an identical wheel (the original had bounded completely off the airfield), hopped into another plane, caught up with the student, and tried to make the fact known by holding up the wheel and making hand signals. Just how much that helped is conjecture. The plane suffered extensive damage on landing, but, fortunately, the pilot was not seriously injured.

The next day, while standing in about the same spot as the day before, I happened to be near a group of instructors discussing the incident when I overheard one of them say, "well I know what I'd have done. As soon as I felt the wing drop, I'd have intentionally ground-looped[11] the plane toward the missing wheel. That would have shifted a lot of weight on to the good wheel, which would have delayed the wing or strut from striking the ground, until a lower speed was reached, thus minimizing the damage."

That statement, though self-aggrandizing in nature, impressed me. I wondered would he have really thought of that during the time of the incident? And would it have worked? I didn't know it then, but I was to find out later.

\* \* \*

At Luke Field, we flew the AT6A, a low-wing monoplane with the usual tandem seating arrangement, and retractable landing gear. It was a marvelous training plane, especially for fighter pilots. Interestingly, the Japanese Zero looked very much like the AT6. In fact, many movies were made with an AT6 used to represent the Japanese Zero.

My first flight in Advanced Training was a 45-minute dual on December 19, 1941. Over the next six weeks, they crammed an unusually heavy flight schedule on us. I didn't mind. I loved it. The weather was great, and

---

[11] Ground looping is where you basically make a partial spin on the ground. It is not a desirable thing to do when you are landing! Damage is almost inevitable.

I loved flying the AT6. During that six-week period there were three days when I flew for more than four hours and two days for about six and $\frac{1}{2}$ hours. For student pilots, that is a load. My last training flight occurred January 27, 1942. It was a five-hour thirty-minute solo night flight. It also was a rather spectacular, though uneventful flight, as I recall.

As part of our training, we flew simulated dogfights. Mostly this involved free-lancing while you try to keep your opponent off your tail or stay on his. Of course, we would not use live ammunition! Actually, there were only a few times we used live ammunition in Advanced Training. They had an instructor fly an AT6 pulling a windsock-like device with a long rope. The pilots tried to shoot the windsock. Obviously, we flew at an angle to the target to make sure we didn't hit the instructor. In addition, we practiced skeet shooting on the ground (with shot guns) to learn how to aim ahead of a moving target. It was designed to help a pilot track another plane. We did a lot of skeet shooting.

I always felt I did pretty well in the air-to-air combat phase -- not the highest, but pretty good. However, I never took unnecessary chances. I was always a conservative pilot.

\* \* \*

I graduated and was commissioned a 2nd Lieutenant on Friday, February 6, 1942, with my parents there, watching. Unfortunately, because of the accelerated nature of all military programs at the time, I saw my parents only one more time before leaving for overseas on July 1st, 1942 and returning in October of 1945.

# STATESIDE

The majority of the graduating class went to Bombing Command, with some going to Training Command, but the cream went to Fighter Command (I say that because I went to Fighter Command, but the truth is I think about everyone was given what they requested).

Orders were written for our group to report to Meridian, Mississippi for duty within seven days. To get there within the required time frame, my good friend, buddy and constant companion since Primary, Bill McGowan, was fortunate to get us a ride with a Port Arthur, Texas Cadet who was one of the few at Cal-Aero with a car. As soon as the graduation ceremonies were over on Friday, February 6, we took off, driving all night and all the next day. This was before there were any Interstate Highways. It was all two-lane roads that weaved their way through every small town and hamlet.

Even though McGowan succeeded in getting us a car ride to Mississippi, he didn't help with the driving. He couldn't. McGowan, who had just been commissioned a pilot in the Army Air Force, did not have a driver's license.

Growing up in Los Angeles, his family never owned a car and he had never learned to drive. Yet here he was, fully qualified to fly fighter aircraft and would be flying P-40's with the rest of us, just as soon as we reached Meridian. Since I had driven cars, trucks, and tractors on the farm since I was 13 years old, it was hard for me to believe he really couldn't drive, but he couldn't.

We arrived in Port Arthur on Saturday night, very tired and ready for bed. We hardly slept at all on the 24-hour drive, nor had we slept much prior to leaving, given it was our graduation. So when we got to Port Arthur, we crashed. We stayed there that night, most of the next day (during which we mostly slept), and Sunday night as well.

We then completed the trip to Meridian the next day.

The Key Field Air Base at Meridian was new[12]. As a matter of fact, most military installations throughout the nation were new at that time, having been hastily built in preparation for the war. The air base had one long north-south runway and a short east-west runway. The N-S runway, which we used 90% of the time, had long open approaches at both ends, but the E-W runway still had electrical high lines that ran along a north-south highway which crossed the east end of the runway. (Key Field is now the Meridian Regional Airport).

The first week to ten days were spent in pseudo ground school. We read manuals, listened to experienced P-40 pilots who told us what to look out for, and tried to memorize everything in the cockpit. It is important to remember our dual training was over. The first flight had to be right. Therefore, for safety sake, it was essential we became completely familiar with everything in the cockpit. We did.

My first flight in the P-40 was made on Thursday, February 19th, 1942. It lasted for an hour. It was also an uneventful flight, but actually my recollection of that flight had more to do with the nose of the airplane than the flight itself. It seemed from where I was sitting in the cockpit, the propeller was an awfully long distance away. No training plane I'd ever flown had a nose even close to being that long. It gave a distracting feeling. Of course, no plane I'd ever flown before had an engine with as much power or provided as much speed. Time and practice would cure

---

[12] Key Field was named after Fred and Al Key who set a world flying endurance record in 1935. A museum in their honor is now at the Meridian Regional Airport.

the distracting feeling.

Meridian was to be our home base for the next two months. During that period, we did a lot of flying. Mostly we practiced combat and formation flying, but we also spent a lot of ground time in Link Trainers working on our instrument flying techniques. Occasionally, to make sure our Link Trainer technique would actually work in the air, we would fly dual in a BT-14 or an AT6, which were kept on the base for that purpose.

The P-40 Warhawk

By U.S. Army (The U.S. Air Force was part of the U.S. Army during World War II, so the Army handled the air during that time.)

Practically all the flights were routine training flights. The routine flights were mostly dull, and I have no recollection of them. But I was involved in three flights that were neither routine nor dull. I'll tell you about them.

The first episode occurred very shortly after we had all reached a comfortable feeling flying the P-40. Lt. W. P. Worley approached Bill McGowan and me and asked if we'd be willing to practice a little formation flying in route to his hometown, near Jackson, Mississippi, which was about 90 miles west of Meridian. He wanted to give his hometown folk a sampling of our buzzing skill. We agreed. It sounded like a fun, delightful break from our usual, dull training program.

Bill took the left wing; I took the right and Worley led the way. We gave his house and town a real nice buzz job, but we were careful not to overdo it. After all, Lt. Worley had family and friends there. But we did enough that I'm sure they knew who was responsible.

After having our fun, we headed for home. But as we neared home base, we couldn't help noticing the big change in the weather since we'd left about an hour earlier. A cold front had moved in from the north and brought with it an enormous ugly looking storm cloud. A call to the tower for landing instructions informed us the wind direction had changed 180 degrees since we left. Now the wind was out of the north. This meant to get into landing position, we would have to fly through the storm, and approach the runway from the south.

For you to fully understand our plight and what happened to us, you need to have a little understanding of the "low frequency" electronic navigational aids used in those days. We did not have radar at that time. The British had it and were perfecting it. But for us, it was still a few months away.

The low frequency system we used required the pilot to listen for the Morse Code, a dot and a dash, (". –"), for an "A," or a dash and a dot, ("– .") for an "N." The map on his lap would then tell him in which quadrant he was located (A or N). Between the A and N quadrants was a small overlapping area in which the pilot would hear a steady solid tone. This was because the ". –"and the "– ." were timed to overlap in such a way as to produce the steady solid tone. This area was known as "being on the beam." The beam would lead the pilot to the destination marked on the map. We all had spent many hours in Link Trainers practicing the system and I think we all felt confident about using it. I did, anyway.

So into the storm cloud we went, not in formation, but one at a time and at different levels to avoid a possible collision. When I got into the storm, I immediately realized we had a problem. Our training program had grossly shortchanged us! No one had ever told me or anyone else as far as I could later learn: this low frequency system would not work in a snowstorm! All I could hear was a very loud, high-pitched squeal. The volume was so loud it was impossible to distinguish anything in the background.

OK, so I wouldn't use the beam system. No big problem in this case. Everything else seemed to be working okay, and I figured the compass was about all I needed anyway, so I turned the radio volume down and headed south. As expected, in less than ten minutes, I broke out into sunshine on the other side and from there all I needed to do was drop down to about 500 feet then slide under the clouds and navigate to the south end of our airport and land, which I did without further incident. A few minutes later W.P. Worley landed and then we waited for McGowan. And we waited, and we waited.

Since he never showed up by nightfall, we figured he must have diverted to an alternate field, or something. But he never called in. We began to worry. We never heard anything the next day, either, or the next. Then the following day, a rumor swept the unit like wildfire. A hunter had found a crashed plane, along with a pilot's body, in the swamp about eight miles from Meridian.

A few minutes later, a Captain from Group Headquarters came by and said, "Come along, Lt. Wait. We need you to make a positive identification." I shouted "NO! Not me! There are fifty guys here that can identify him, get one of them to do it. I don't want to see him!"

"You're his best friend," the Captain answered, "and we want a positive identification. So come along. That's an order!"

This was the toughest thing I ever had to do. His body had already been brought to the morgue and you can have no idea how much I hated to see them pull that drawer out. It was McGowan, all right. Fortunately, they had cleaned him up a lot, but he was still a mess. He had hit old Mother Earth at a very high rate of speed.

The Captain suggested we go out to the crash site and see if we could learn anything. A guide was needed to find it. We had to walk a good distance from the nearest road, and through a lot of pine trees. Then, there it was -- a giant crater in the soft, mostly sandy soil, with just the tail of a P-40 sticking out. Nothing else was visible, except McGowan's parachute, which was still attached to the tail.

As best as we could figure, Bill must have become disoriented, panicked, lost control, and bailed out. He might have lived to a ripe old age, had he not pulled his ripcord so quickly. By opening it immediately, it allowed the parachute to get caught on the tail of the plane. The plane went straight down, obviously at a very high rate of speed, dragging poor McGowan with it.

I've often wondered had Bill McGowan learned to drive a car as a teenager, would it have carried over and helped his decision-making skill as a pilot? I have a picture hanging in my office that was taken when we visited the Hollywood "Keep 'Em Flying" studio together in September 1941. I still look at it and wonder.

* * *

Roughly two weeks after McGowan's death, another flight of an entirely different nature gave me quite a thrill, like a carnival ride. Fortunately, its conclusion was different too.

Actually, it was a routine training flight, or at least, it started out that way. Lt. Farabee and I were on an instrument flying check using an AT6. When airborne, the pilot in the rear seat goes under a hood so the only thing he can see is the instrument panel. Then he executes a series of maneuvers and navigational tests with the pilot in the front seat observing and making sure no accidents happen. I rode the front seat on the first flight and when Lt. Farabee indicated he was finished with his 'under the hood program,' I took over the flying.

Things had been rather dull and routine, even boring, since McGowan's death, and I just felt like spicing things up a bit. Down below, I spotted a long military convoy of trucks and jeeps slowly winding its way through the pine covered hillsides and I decided to give them a good buzz job. I did, and did it pretty well, too, if I do say so myself. The prop was put in a lower pitch so the engine would make a lot of noise, then I made two extremely low passes from the front and two from the rear, then headed straight for home base where we landed and exchanged seats.

Now it was my turn to go under the hood. After about thirty minutes under the hood, I indicated to Lt. Farabee that my routine was finished, and he could take us home. He did much better than that. He took us right down the Main Street of Meridian at such a low altitude, I was looking up to see people looking down from second story windows, watching us fly by! Naturally, he had the prop in low pitch for maximum noise affect. With the sound bouncing back and forth off the buildings, it made quite a racket. Meanwhile, I was sitting in the back seat saying to myself, "Dear God, I sure hope this idiot researched this stunt before pulling it off, because if there are any cables stretched across any intersection, as is often the case, we're a couple of dead Lieutenants." I had to admit, if his aim was to top me, he did. The ride was quite a thrill, and apparently the Mayor and most City Councilmen got a good rise from it too. They and several citizens called the airbase to tell the commander just how much they enjoyed it!! In fact, we were told later the switchboard at the airbase was so jammed with calls they couldn't handle them.

When we landed, the Commanding Officer sent an emissary to tell us to report to him immediately. The upshot was, Lt. Farabee was grounded for six days and I was grounded for three. We both had been doing a lot of flying and I needed a little rest, anyway. Actually, we knew with the war going on, and the need for trained pilots, nothing very severe would happen to us. Yes, we probably were getting a little cocky, but then, on the other hand, we may also have begun to pick up a few saddle sores from the concentrated and uninterrupted training program for the past nine weeks, with no end in sight.

Apparently, the High Command came to the same conclusion. According to my flight logbook, a short-term time-out was called between 3-16 and 3-26. I am sure I went home for a visit, between those dates, but at this time, 58 years later, I haven't the faintest recollection of any part of the visit, except for the trip back from Wichita. I can recall the airliner landing at Shreveport. That's all I remember. Why I would recall the Shreveport landing and remember nothing else about the trip, I can't explain.

\* \* \*

Roughly three weeks after returning from that short vacation, we had one of those rare days when the wind was blowing directly from the west, with enough force that the N-S runway was deemed unsafe to use. The crosswind would have been too strong. As usual, I was flying that day. We were doing combat flying drills. Nothing exciting about that, we did it a lot. The excitement occurred when we came into land. Landing to the westward on the E-W runway meant all planes had to clear the high-line wires that still blocked the end of the runway. I wasn't particularly fearful of them, but I certainly respected them. I knew they were there. They were easy to see, and I knew they could be dangerous if struck. But for some stupid reason (mental lapse) I played my approach a little lower and slower than I should have.

I can recall the final approach I made that day quite vividly. I had one eye on the high-line wires and another eye on the air speed indicator. I was intent on keeping the speed low because of the short runway, but just above stalling speed. Until the last second it appeared the approach was timed perfect. Then suddenly I feared my tail might snag the top wire, so I pulled up ever so slightly. After clearing the wire, I relaxed and allowed the plane to drop into flaring[13] out position. Unfortunately, I was so close to stalling speed the plane didn't flare like it usually does. Consequently, the wheels made fairly solid contact with the runway. Since there was no bounce, I was surprised when I felt the left wing droop and realized my left landing gear was not locked into its down position.

On P-40s, the wheels retract straight back. When the wheels are lowered, a small pin drops into place. That locks the wheels in an extended position. If this pin is sheered, as mine was, the wheel dangles loosely, like a broken (and useless) leg.

As soon as I felt the left wing droop, I knew what happened, and my mind raced for a solution. The force of the touchdown had obviously caused the pin to sheer. At first, my instinct was to gun the engine and get airborne again so I could redo my landing, but I immediately dis-

---

[13] Flaring: When you are coming in for a landing, the nose of the plane is pointing up slightly. When you get to about 10 feet from the ground, there is a cushion of air forming underneath the plane. You want to time it so that your stalling speed is reached just as the wheels touch. When you get close to the ground, you raise the nose "Flaring out" so that you are rounding out the bottom, you are actually floating on the compressed air between the wings and the ground until you reach the stalling speed.

missed that. What would be the point? I realized I would still have to land on one wheel, and I would also have to come in over the wire again. That would be pretty stupid, I realized quickly, as I was already on the ground!

In my earphones, I could hear the tower operator shouting that my left wheel was not down and locked. All at the same time, my mind was racing back to Primary, when the student had lost a wheel, and immediately I knew what had to be done.

For three or four seconds, I was able to hold the left wing up using maximum aileron controls. Then, as the left wing started to droop again, I hit the left rudder pedal. Hard! The plane slowly veered left off the runway into a grassy area, which fortunately was level and smooth. Quickly, I coasted to a stop. I pulled the canopy back, and just sat there. I didn't even turn the idling engine off. I knew it was all right, but I wasn't. I was thoroughly disgusted with myself and was in no hurry to get out, or to do anything. I'm the guy that makes more perfect landings than anyone, remember? Well I just spoiled my perfect record and just demonstrated that perhaps I'm not as good as I thought I was. Or more likely I got a little careless and sloppy.

Suddenly, I became aware someone was standing on the wing, by my open canopy, shouting: "Are you all right, Lieutenant? Are you all right?" That's when I first noticed the ambulance and fire truck. "Yeah, sure, I'm O.K., just disgusted with myself, that's all!" Thereupon, I turned off the idling engine and climbed out.

As with all accidents, there was an investigation. But in this case, I came out smelling like a rose. The highline wires got a very bad report, but I didn't. Even the damage to the airplane turned out to be minimal. The maintenance officer came by and said he wanted to shake my hand. He said, "Lieutenant, do you realize there was only one inch clearance between the propeller tips and the ground, but they never touched? That was the big thing!

Had the propeller tips touched the ground, we'd have had to pull the engine and take it apart or replace the engine with a new one. The wing damage is easy to handle. In fact, we could have this plane flying again in 24 hours. I don't know how you did it!" I told him and the investigating officer the Cal-Aero Primary student story.

It is not known if there was any real connection, but a week later, without warning, we all (pilots, personal belongings, and planes) were moved to Orlando, FL on Tuesday, April 13th. Trucks hauled the personal belongings and we pilots flew the P-40s.

Orlando was actually a nice place to move to. The airport was larger, nicer, and close to a much better town. Orlando even had a big party (dance) for us with a big band and the whole works. Of course, this was years before Disney came to town. Orlando was considerably smaller then.

It was in Orlando we were first introduced to the new navigational tool, RADAR[14]. Initially, we had a lot of problems with it. It seemed like we would get a lot of reciprocal headings (180 degrees wrong), but we quickly learned to appreciate its dead accuracy when it was right. Later models were free of the early bugs and worked considerably better.

What I remember most about Orlando is that Lt. Smithers and I, while walking past a used car lot one evening, impulsively went together and bought a second-hand

---

[14] "**RADAR**" is actually an anacronym. It stood for "**RA**dio Detection **A**nd **R**anging"

1932 Model B Ford for fifty bucks. We were tired of walking and taking cabs into town. Unfortunately, the car wasn't big enough to handle all the other pilots who wanted to ride. Finally, to solve the dilemma, we willed the car to Jack Martin's (not his real name) wife, Janet, who was the only wife in the squadron. She kept it and did all the driving, and we scheduled rides thru her. If the car was crowded, sometimes poor Jack was left behind. Whatever happened to that car, I do not recall, but I believe Janet drove the car to our next base assignment, and from there, to the auto graveyard.

1932 Model B
From Wikipedia

We were at Orlando only for about four weeks to mid-May, when suddenly the Pentagon decided we weren't going to fly the P-40. Why, I never learned. But that's the way the military does its best work. They never confuse you with logic and reasoning. You're just given orders instead. In layman's language that meant that "you are going to Wilmington, NC. We have P-39s waiting for you there."

Talk about rustic living. Wilmington was it. We slept in tents back in a forest of beautiful pine trees. For the outdoor lover, it made for a picture postcard setting, with the Atlantic Ocean beckoning. It was very nice. Regrettably, we were to be there for only three weeks before being moved again.

For those of you who have never heard of the P-39, I think a brief description is in order.

Bell P-39 Q Airacobra
USAF Museum

The P-39 had a unique design. For starters, the engine was behind the pilot, rather than in front like most prop planes. A long shaft ran between the pilot's legs from the engine to the propeller. This shaft served a dual purpose. Not only did it transfer the motor's energy to the prop, it was hollow and also served as the barrel for a 37 mm cannon. This design suggested the chief use of the P-39 would be as an anti-tank weapon.

Another feature, which all pilots liked, was the tricycle landing gear. While the P-39 was approximately the same size and weight as the P-40, its appearance and flight characteristics were significantly different.

Even prior to my first flight, I had heard rumors the plane possessed strange flight characteristics. For example, I heard the P-39 had been known to tumble (end-over-end) in flight.

I never really believed the stories because it just didn't sound logical. It sounded more like an old wives' tale. I reasoned if the plane had speed enough to fly, it just could not possibly happen. Nevertheless, I was inclined to concede there was a slight possibility it might happen if the plane was ever in an unusual, stalled, non-flying situation.

Well, I decided if I am going to be flying this alba-
tross in combat, for my own sake, I had better find out for
sure. Having experienced firsthand knowledge of the man-
nerisms and flight characteristics of the plane you are
flying is very important to a pilot. So on the second flight I
ever made with the P-39, I decided to take it up to above
10,000 feet (this was to give me plenty of room to bail out
if things got completely out of hand) and I started putting
the plane through all manner of stalls,[15] from different positions, power on and power off, then followed this with
several more severe speedier maneuvers. No aerodynamic
problems were encountered that I couldn't handle, but I
suddenly became aware that my engine was racing. This
isn't supposed to happen. The RPM for a constant speed
prop is controlled by a setting provided by the pilot and
remains constant regardless of the throttle setting. This
means that the engine automatically adjusts the pitch of
the propeller so that the RPM stays the same (the RPM of
the engine – not the forward speed of the plane). I pulled
the throttle back and with some experimentation, realized
I had a propeller locked in low pitch.[16] That's tantamount

---

[15] **Stalling:** Stalling a plane means flying it so slow that it loses the lift
on the wing. That is, there is not enough airflow going over the wings
to give the plane enough lift to stay in the air. The result is that the
plane starts to drop out of control! Hopefully, the pilot can gain lift –
prior to reaching the ground – or else...

[16] **Propeller Pitch:** Pitch in propeller is same idea as gears in a car,
only done electronically or with hydraulics not gears. The actual angle
of the propeller blade changes, so it batters more or less air. Low pitch
is used to take off for maximum power. When you are in low pitch, you

to driving a car or truck in low gear. Not knowing whether I was in trouble or not (and not having any interest in further experimentation to find out), I decided it was time to head for home base, which I could see off in the distance.

A call to the tower alerted them to my situation and I requested they give me a landing priority. I also asked that they keep other planes from the area until I'd landed. They complied. (You see, I didn't want any rubbernecking Sunday afternoon type sightseers getting in my way, forcing me to detour, or to change speed or altitude. That might have been enough to louse things up, since I was fearful a level flight could not be maintained). Actually, it turned out to be an easy, smooth flight in. After all, it was downhill all the way. I started from over 10,000 feet and ended with another perfect landing.

That evening, a manufacturer's representative came around to our tent, asking for me. Then he proceeded to ask me, in front of the other pilots, if I would agree to make some changes in the numbers on my flight log re-

---

would set your RPM at 3,000 or so. After you take off, the pitch of the propeller would change to maintain a constant RPM. Once you are up to 2,000 to 3,000 feet, you would lower RPM to about 2,000, but increase the pitch. At cruising speed, you would change the pitch into high pitch, which would lower the engine's RPM and may be able to improve gas mileage. When you get to your destination, you usually put it into low pitch before landing. In this way, if you run into trouble and must abort the landing, you would have maximum power to allow you to gain altitude quickly.

When I had the problem with the P-39, the gismo to automatically adjust the pitch failed to compensate, which caused the plane's engine to race. The plane had locked into low pitch. I was concerned that I would not have enough power.

port. (All pilots are required to make a written report after each flight). He said their wind tunnel tests were unable to duplicate the numbers I reported. The inference was not exactly complimentary, and I got a little testy. After all, I've always taken pride in being precise and accurate in my work (I still am). I explained "I wasn't flying in a wind tunnel, I was flying at more than 10,000 feet over North Carolina doing several different experimental maneuvers, and I was paying very close attention to my instruments and knew exactly what they were recording, and what I reported on my log sheet was exactly what they showed."

He went away a little unhappy, to say the least. The impression left with me was that the Air Force had been applying some heat to his company (Bell Aircraft) and I'm sure it probably had to do with an accumulation of a lot of matters, not just my flight.

After he departed, a large group of pilots who had been standing among the tall pine trees listening very attentively gave me a very enthusiastic standing ovation.

We weren't at Wilmington very long. Around the first of June, we were relocated to Manchester, New Hampshire, still flying P-39s. This time though, we were flying them with belly tanks. The belly tanks were to provide us with enough fuel to fly the Atlantic, in steps or stages. The stages were Goose Bay – Greenland – Iceland – Scotland. Naturally, we needed a little practice time because the belly tanks not only increased the gross weight of the plane, it also changed its flying characteristics. So each day, we took off and flew around the area. Nothing fancy, just getting used to the different feel of the aircraft. Then about the fourth day it happened. Yep, my prop locked in a fixed position again, only this time it was in full high-pitch. Of the two positions, I think full low-pitch is preferable, but I'd much rather have it working right! Again, I made it in safely and made a good landing (of course), but this time no manufacturer's rep came calling.

We continued daily practice flying right up to mid-

June. The final briefing was held the evening before we were to depart. The weather people were there and gave us a favorable forecast for our flight. All the Brass were there as well, along with the B-17 pilots who were to lead the way and do the navigating, and, of course, all the 52nd Fighter Group P-39 pilots. Right in the middle of the briefing, Col. Allison, a full colonel and the commanding officer of the 52nd Group, had to leave the stage. (I think Col. Allison was a West Point Graduate for he was a tough nut). He'd received an emergency call from the Pentagon during the briefing. He returned to the stage a short while later and announced that we should go back to our rooms -- the flight was cancelled. We were going to Ft. Dix in New Jersey, instead, and put aboard a ship. We should arrive in Great Britain sometime in early July. We were never given an explanation for the sudden change in plans. (The P-39s were apparently deemed unworthy craft for the European Theater).

We left the States on June 30th, aboard the "Duchess of Bedford" troop ship (formerly a luxury liner) in a very large naval convoy. Throughout the trip, the "Duchess" was positioned immediately behind the battleship Texas. (Of course, I had no idea I would see the ship again in action or one day live in its namesake). The "Duchess" was equipped with one large anti-aircraft gun but had no gunners to operate it. Military logic said the pilots of the 52nd Fighter Group aboard the ship would make good ship-based gunners, since they'd had extensive training in aerial gunnery. Do you recall what happened to me the night of Pearl Harbor? Well it happened again. Only this time, we didn't have the benefit of California weather.

I've never been so cold in my life as I was that night being topside, manning that AA gun. This was after about five days at sea and the convoy must have been as near to the North Pole as it could possibly get, for even with wearing all the clothes I owned, including my flying uniform, I was still freezing cold.

Also aboard the "Duchess" was a hospital group, commanded by Gen. Roosevelt (another one of the successful Roosevelt boys). Most of the group's personnel consisted of nurses, who, by a unanimous vote of the 52nd Fighter Group pilots, were the ugliest, homeliest group of young women ever assembled in one spot. How could we be so unlucky? Then a miraculous transformation took place after about five days at sea. We discovered we'd misjudged them. Indeed, there were several very attractive gals in that group. Apparently, the pilots had an identical effect on the nurses. Each day the two groups got friendlier. But fortunately, or unfortunately, however one would be inclined to look at it, the physical facilities of a jam-packed troop ship with no unoccupied spaces, prevented courtship from going beyond togetherness out on the open deck. But there was a lot of togetherness on deck. A few of the couples did manage to find their way into lifeboats or a vacant stairwell, but they were often discovered by the MPs. The ship was very cramped. There was only about two feet height between the bunks in the quarters.

When we arrived at Liverpool, around July 8th, the Hospital Group went their way to a base in the London area and the 52nd Fighter Group went in the opposite direction to Londonderry, North Ireland. That ended a beautiful flowering relationship for many of the guys. Not for me, though. I was friendly with two or three of the girls, but nothing serious developed.

# LONDONDERRY

Arriving at our base near Londonderry on July 9th, we found our new planes waiting for us. Well, calling these planes "new" is like calling the pyramids 'new'. They were "new" only in the sense we'd never flown Spitfires before. In actuality, these planes were about as old as Methuselah. Well, maybe not quite that old, but close. They might not have had the years, but they certainly had the wear. They had been through the Battle of Britain (1940), which made them about two years older than the P-40s and P-39s we left behind. In fairness, I believe the Spitfire was probably a better fighter plane.[17] It was light-

---

17 **The Reason We Got Spitfires.** The following was found on the internet (www.star-games.com/exhibits/spitfire/spitops.html). It comes from a report entitled "History of USAAF Spitfire Operations in the Mediterranean (31st and 52nd Fighter Groups)".

"... There were several reasons that the 31st and 52nd left their P-39 aircraft in the U.S. to pick up Spitfires in the U.K. The first of these reasons has to do with capability of the P-39.

"The P-39 lacked two vital performance characteristics needed for operations in the European theater. During the summer of 1942 as bombers and fighters began to assemble-in England, much of the fighter combat took place at high altitudes, and escorting bombers required a long-range capability, neither of which the P-39 had. The British thought it would be unwise to pit the P-39 against the Luftwaffe's better performing aircraft. In the opinion of many pilots that flew them, the P-39 was the worst fighter aircraft built by the Americans in World War II.

"General Henry H. "Hap" Arnold was anxious to get American fighter units into the European theater in the summer of 1942 to escort the B-17 bombers about to begin bombing missions over the continent. With that in mind, a bold plan to fly the P-39s across the Atlantic Ocean was worked out, to be led by B-17s via a newly-devised northern short-hop route. This would be the first time fighter aircraft had ever attempted such a crossing. General Arnold expected to lose 25 percent of the fighters on this ferry attempt, a figure considered by some to be conservative." *(We certainly weren't aware of this! Makes me kind of glad we didn't take them across.)*

"The 31 FG pilots had been practicing long-range missions with belly tanks out of Grenier Field, New Hampshire in mid-May, flying 800-mile round-trip flights to Washington, D.C. and back. They were running into several problems. These included stalls caused by fuel sloshing around in partially filled belly tanks, and loss of aircraft control at-slow airspeeds while trying to fly formation on B-17s going in and out of the weather.

"An unexpected solution to the problems of the P-39 presented itself in 1942. With the Battle of Britain over, the loss rate for Spitfires declined dramatically. Britain was producing more Spitfires than the Royal Air Force (RAF) needed. The decision was finally made that the ocean crossing by P-39s would be abandoned. Instead a reverse lease-lend program was established, and the RAF supplied Spitfires to two American fighter groups. On arrival in the United Kingdom, the 31st Fighter Group and 52nd Fighter Group began training in their new unit equipment, the Spitfire."

*This report went on to say that* "Overall, the pilots of the 31 FG and 52 FG were very pleased flying the Spitfire. The aircraft was considered easy to fly but was most difficult to taxi. Part of the problem was going from the tricycle landing gear configuration of the P-39 to a tail-dragger configuration on the Spitfire. Combine that difference with the unusual braking system found on the Spitfire and inexperienced pilots tended to ground loop the aircraft taxiing or on landing. This often resulted in wing-tip damage as a minimum." *I find it interesting this report fails to mention the fact we received old and beat-up Spitfires, not new ones off the assembly line. And the fact a lot of the American Pilots were very discouraged by this. We certainly weren't happy with the Spitfires!*

er, more maneuverable, and had a faster climb rate. Trouble is these particular planes were not fit for combat. They were not even safe to fly. They were worn out and had been very poorly maintained, mechanically. That may sound like we didn't get off to a real good start. Truthfully, we didn't.

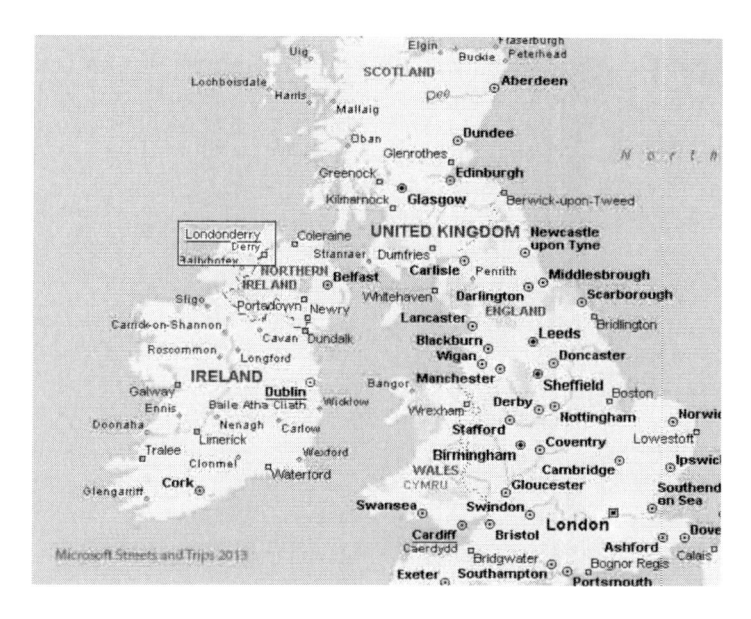

Right from the beginning at Londonderry, the moral of the 52nd Fighter Group started out low and went down from there. Besides having to fly old, unsafe planes, a lot of other factors were involved, some minor, some not. But it all accumulated to have a powerful negative effect on our outlook. You might not think of them as important, but if you had been there, I suspect you'd have been bitching along with everyone else. Here are some of the factors I'm referring to:

**1. Communications**: The British objected to the way we talked on the radio to the tower and other radio centers. Brits were using terms like "Over and Out."

American terminology was quite different, less formal sounding. Being military guests, we had to adopt the British system.

**2. Food**: At Londonderry, we ate what the British ate. Mostly this meant smelly fish or smellier mutton. Even the preparation was bad. Cooks could ruin what otherwise might have been tasty food. No one asked for seconds. The food stunk. It either tasted bad or was completely tasteless. I don't know of a single dish the Americans would say, "oh this is good." None of us liked Brussels Sprouts, for example, although eventually many of us developed a taste out of necessity. Not very helpful was the American supplement of powdered eggs, powdered milk, SPAM, and "K" rations.

**3. Transportation:** On American bases, jeeps were used to transport people (pilots). But the British bases used bicycles. As a result we rode bicycles. There were no jeeps.

**4. Reading Matter**: The only daily paper to read came from London, England. It was full of marvelous things the British military was accomplishing. Americans got little mention, and when they did, it was usually with a less than flattering slant. Several months later, the "Stars and Stripes," a paper written for and by GI's, came into existence. It was a tremendous help, but it came much too late for us.

**5. Press Coverage**: Because we weren't flying American planes, our own American press virtually ignored us. In letters I received from home, my mother informed me they had read nothing in the daily Wichita paper about American pilots flying Spitfires in Northern Ireland. I do recall an AP reporter being at our base one day, but he left. He was it.

**6. Entertainment:** Londonderry was a depressing place to be located. Entertainment was limited and frankly, not very interesting. Had we been located near London, I'm sure moral would have been better. I can recall having one date. Never asked for another. My date, as did nearly all the girls I saw there, had a repulsive disfigurement. Her legs looked like fence posts. No ankles.

**7. Weather:** While I was there, it rained every day. That's the truth. Every single day. It may have been only a five-minute shower, but it rained. To you, it might not sound very depressing. Here in Texas, it might even be considered a blessing -- especially in July. But to a pilot yearning to fly, miles from home and already pissed off, it was miserable. It was also a tremendous annoyance when trying to get in flying assignments. On the flip side, it did keep the countryside beautifully green and fresh looking.

After giving you seven good supplementary reasons for our moral problem, I must get back to what was really bugging our pilots (especially me) the most: the old planes and our perceived second-class status.

For starters, when we first left the States, we all made assumptions that turned out to be incorrect. Naturally, we believed we were being sent to the European theater to engage the German's in aerial warfare. But our being located in Londonderry, a spot that is physically as far from London as Frankfort, Germany, pretty much negated that. Obviously, we weren't being counted on to defend England or to make any other meaningful contributions we could see. Even more ego shattering was the realization we were considered second-teamers, or second-raters. We get the Royal Air Force's (RAF) hand-me-downs, while they received new Spitfires. It also hurt knowing our American High Command obviously agreed to this arrangement. It was evident who was calling the shots.

We didn't really have a clear mission while stationed there, either. At least none us pilots could see. Once in a while we would fly escort duty for the massive convoys coming over from the States. But these missions were not very exciting as nothing ever happened. All of this contributed to the low morale.

Each pilot flew the same aircraft full time. He also had the same crew chief (mechanic) and parked his plane in the same revetment (an embankment of earth surrounding the parking space).

Flying the same plane each time is more comforting to the pilot. Like breaking in a new pair of shoes, you get used to it. In short, it helps lower the anxiety level. Then there is the matter of the pilot and crew chief becoming sufficiently at ease with each other to work somewhat as teammates toward repair and maintenance problems. That's definitely a plus. I will give a personal example, which wasn't exactly a run-of-the-mill, or average case, but you'll get the point.

It was nearing mid-August when I made one particular flight in a Spitfire that was so full of tension and gut-wrenching emotion, it was instrumental in changing my Army Air Force career. It started out routinely, just like many others. I wanted to do some work on my combat training exercises and was putting my plane through a series of fairly violent maneuvers (wringing it out) when I suddenly noticed a collection of heavy, thick oil on my windshield. In fact, as I watched, it rapidly got thick enough that I couldn't see out the windshield.

A little oil on a windshield is not too unusual. With the force of a very strong slipstream, it either blows off entirely or is reduced to a non-factor spot. As a matter of fact, in more sophisticated planes a thin film of very light oil is intentionally ejected onto the windscreen to prevent the collection of ice. But in such cases, the pilot's vision is never impaired.

This case though was different. This oil (or grease) was a murky, muddy dark brown compound that clung tightly to the windscreen with such tenacity and thickness that it was like glue. Visibility through the windshield was reduced to zero. Some oil even started covering the canopy sides and top. Obviously, I was in trouble. Just how seriously, I wasn't sure. I knew as a last ditch option, I could always bail out, but that didn't appeal to me (both from a standpoint of pride and remembering what happened to my best friend, Bill McGowan) and before opting for that, I wanted to make at least one pass at a landing attempt.

Whenever an emergency landing is to be attempted, the first order of business is to call the tower and advise them of the situation. This I did, and I also asked for clearance to make an emergency straight-in landing approach. It, too, was granted. Next, I pulled the canopy back and determined after some experimenting that I could see at roughly a 40 degree angle ahead by looking out through the open side, but I had to be careful not to get my face too close to the slipstream, or it could cause permanent blindness. My biggest worry was being absolutely certain I was correctly aligned with the runway. Anyway, considering the alternative, I decided it was worth a try, so down I went.

What I have just recounted, I remember quite well. The surprising thing is, I have no recollection whatsoever of the actual landing itself. So perhaps the actual landing wasn't as scary as I thought it was going to be. At any rate, it was a safe one and I'm still alive. (Undoubtedly, another one of my perfect landings.) Notwithstanding, what transpired during the next couple of hours was even more gut wrenching. That period of time is imprinted on my mind like it happened yesterday, even though it was almost sixty years ago.

After parking my plane in its revetment and completing the log report, I mounted my bicycle and headed for the pilot's ready room. The entrance to the pilot's ready room is restricted to pilots only. No exceptions.

As I recall, our room had a pool table and several small tables with chairs for cards or other games to be played. That particular day, I engaged another pilot in a game of cribbage, which we never finished. Actually, I don't believe I've ever played cribbage since that day.

We were playing our game at a table near the rear

of the room, when suddenly I hear one of the fellows near the front door calling out to me, "Hey Wait, your crew chief is here at the front door and wants to talk to you!"

When I got outside, my crew chief said "Lieutenant, about that oil leak, I've found the cause and it's one of the darndest things I've ever seen or heard of. It's so rare, I thought maybe you might like to come see it for yourself."

"Can't you fix it?"

"Yes, sir. I can fix it."

"Well, fix it then." I said. "Why would I want to see it?"

"Well, Sir," he replied, "I don't think you understand. Like I said, this is something I've never heard of happening, but an hour or so ago, in addition to sweating out a landing with all that oil on your windshield, you were in an extremely dangerous situation. In fact, your life was literally hanging by a thread, so to speak. And I just thought, before I fixed it, you'd like to see for yourself just how close you really came to not being with us right now!"

He had successfully stirred my curiosity. "I'll get my bicycle. I'll be right with you." I said. If it was his intention to get my full-undivided attention, he sure got it! I asked for no more details, for it occurred to me from his approach, he wanted to surprise me. Okay then, let's go. I wanted to know what he was talking about.

As an aside, I may have sounded a little testy or irritable when I spoke so sharply to my crew chief, "Well fix it then! Why would I want to see it?" The truth is, I really was irritated. I'll admit it. I had just survived a very tension-filled flight and was very much in need of relaxation and rest. In all honesty, I wasn't much interested in seeing his loose fitting oil filter cap, or a broken oil line, which is what I had assumed caused the problem. Our entire unit had already been exposed to several other maintenance problems.

Whether I apologized to my crew chief for having talked to him so sharply, I do not remember. Probably not.

He was there, though, when I parked the plane. He witnessed the mess, and he saw how shaken I was when I climbed out of the cockpit, so I'm sure he understood. Bear in mind, this flight was much more frightening to me than was the flight I had back in CPT when I landed a lightweight plane in a gale-force wind. At Ft. Hays, I wasn't frightened, because I knew I had the plane under control and there was little doubt in my mind as to how it would end.

In this instance, there had been an abundance of doubt. Because I couldn't see forward, I had to look side to side and just guess and hope that my Spitfire was correctly lined up with the runway. Then I had to use the same technique and guess at when to flare out for a landing while hoping I wasn't overshooting the whole field. All these decisions being made while traveling at about 100 mph. Trust me, it was nerve-wracking. My mind harbored plenty of doubt as to how it would end. That's what made it scary. But what I was about to see was even more frightening.

As we peddled up to the taxi ramp, I could see my plane up ahead (where I'd parked it), facing outward from the revetment toward the taxi ramp, with the plane's nose cone removed and with a step ladder set at the front of the plane.

After parking our bicycles, he said, "Sir, do you see that big nut up there that holds the propeller in place? Well, get up on that ladder here and take a real good look at it. I've put the nut back exactly as I found it.

"You will notice it's almost completely unscrewed. There is only one thread left holding it in place. If that nut makes one turn more, it comes off. Next, the propeller goes flying off into space.

"Sir, I'd say you were damn lucky you didn't try for a second go around approach and got on the ground when you did, wouldn't you?"

Yes, I had been lucky. Very lucky.

Sleep was a little fitful that night. How long would I have lasted, I wondered, if I was in a dogfight with a German and the propeller of my plane suddenly went into low pitch and stayed there like what happened to me two months ago? Or, what would happen if it slipped into full high pitch like last month? Or, even more current a propeller that nearly comes completely off, like today? That's three dead duck cases in two months, all involving propellers. I wouldn't have had a chance in any one of them, no matter how skillful I might have been as a pilot. And really, I had great confidence in my flying skill. I thought my record showed that. Truthfully, I felt my CPT instructor had it right when he wrote in my logbook: "Very apt, one of the best." Being a competitive person, I honestly believed I could hold my own in a flying skill contest with anyone.

As I lay there in bed thinking about it, it occurred to me perhaps two of those three failures might have been my own fault. As I recalled, at least two propeller failures occurred on flights in which I was "wringing it out," or putting the plane through a series of extremely harsh maneuvers to test the plane's limitations as well as my own. Very strong gyroscopic pressure is generated from a spinning propeller. Perhaps, I reasoned, those high-speed tight turns and experimental skidding flip-flop U-turns executed while simulating dog fight action, created a force exceeding the propeller's designed limitation. Who knows? That might explain one of the two cases involving the P-39s. In any case, it would never explain what happened with the Spitfire. That is a proven plane. It was a smashing success in the Battle of Britain. The most plausible answer in this case is that the plane was simply old and had amassed too many flying hours, plus it was in a poor state maintenance-wise. All these thoughts led up to an even bigger question. How come my country even gave us these old planes to fly and supposedly to fight with, in the first place?

Yes, my country did agree to that. And for years, our country has led us to believe its fighting men were equipped with the latest and best fighting equipment. Apparently, use of second-hand and obsolete airplanes loaned by a friendly power doesn't count. With that non-comforting thought, I finally went to sleep.

Flying the next morning did not appeal to me. Suddenly, flying was no longer fun. Formerly, it was lots of fun. I loved it from the very first and was always impatient to get to the flight line and get airborne. But this day was different. The enthusiasm was gone. 'Maybe the location is at fault,' I thought, 'or the lousy weather. It rains too much here. But today, I'm glad it's raining. It makes a good excuse not to fly.'

That afternoon, Col. Allison called the 52nd Fighter Group pilots together and addressed the moral problem, head on. It was evident he was well aware of the problem and apparently, he had been discussing the matter with the 8th Air Force Headquarters. He wound up his address by saying the 8th Air Force had authorized him to say that a limited number of transfers could be arranged for those wanting out. He said his office door would remain open for the next 24 hours, solely to discuss the issue with individual pilots. Anyone wanting to talk with him about it should walk right in.

Okay, now I had a new and unexpected problem. While an opportunity had been offered to get out, I wasn't sure I really wanted out. Complicating matters even more was I still might not be allowed out, even if I asked for it. Col. Allison had said there were a limited number of transfers. Exactly how many, does "limited" mean? Further compounding the dilemma was the time factor. A decision had to be made within 24 hours, leaving little time to procrastinate. Actually, the decision would be a lot easier if not for the stressful thought of becoming permanently separated from a good gang of pilots. We had been together, not only as fellow pilots, but also as buddies and friends, as part of class 42B for over a year. We had been through a lot together (flying school, P40s, P39s, and now Spitfires). It was odd, how at a time like this, I would think of McGowan! I wished he were here. I would have liked to talk to him. He always pumped me up.

That evening, about two hours after his meeting, I walked by Col. Allison's office. The door was open, and Col. Allison was at his desk, working or reading, but he was alone. I walked on by. I still had the upcoming night to think about it, and I felt I needed it.

I didn't sleep well again that night. I kept going over everything in my head. I was not happy there – and I really resented our country for giving us these rejects for planes. I didn't talk over my dilemma with anyone, however. It was a decision I felt I had to make alone. It was a rough night.

The next morning, I peeked in Col. Allison's open door. Again he was alone. I walked in, saluted, was invited to be at ease, and directed to sit down.


There were eight of us on the Londonderry railway platform several days later. Four of us were from the 52nd Fighter Group and the other four from the 31st Fighter Group. The 31st Fighter Group was composed of class 42A pilots that had been stationed at a base just across the river from us. They had arrived in Northern Ireland three weeks before we did and had also been flying the same old Spitfires. Like me, they all had mixed feelings, but all were grateful they had written orders in their pockets, transferring them to the 8th Air Force Headquarters for reassignment.

What new assignments were given the four pilots from the 31st, I do not know. I did not know them personally prior to meeting them on that platform, and I made no effort to keep in touch. Of the remaining three, I knew Lts. Gabriel and Thibedeau the best, and I stayed in touch with them. Lt. Gabriel was assigned to the 27th Ferry and Transport Squadron. He managed to get himself checked out on about every type of plane in England and was frequently given the task of flying VIPs (such as Bob Hope, Bing Crosby, Glenn Miller etc.) around Great Britain. Little did I know then that I too would later have something to do with the 27th. (Glen Miller, by the way, vanished while being flown around England during the war. He was in a C-64, which was a Canadian plane, but it was flown by one of the pilots from the 27th. The C-64 was a high-wing monoplane that would seat about five people. I did not know the pilot who flew the plane that fateful day. I believe I was at Southport when Glen Miller disappeared forever.)

Watching TV from our home in Prairie Village, Kansas in the mid-1950s, I was startled at my first sight of a professional entertainer that looked enough like Lt. Gabriel to be an identical twin. It was Liberace! Even more astonishing was his voice. It likewise sounded exactly like the Lt. Gabriel I knew. And their voices were very distinctive. Could they actually be the same guy? Hardly.

The Lt. Gabriel I knew, displayed absolutely no musical talents, nor displayed any flashy tendencies (of course in the military during WWII, nobody could). He just loved flying airplanes and he was good at it. Furthermore, he spent his free time chasing girls and he was good at that too. But then there is a very conclusive reason they couldn't be the same guy. The Lt. Gabriel I knew, in 1946, fatally flew into the side of Mt. Ranier while attempting to ferry a C-54 to a base in the Northwest.

To the best of my knowledge, Lt. Thibedeau was the only one to actually return to the 52nd Fighter Group, although I came close. Approximately two months after we left, we learned the 52nd had been relocated to a base in Southern England, (Biggin Hill) not far from London. This made social visits with our old buddies possible. Lt. Thibedeau, who I believe missed them more than I did, decided to go for a visit and returned with the exciting news that they had been completely re-outfitted with the new, latest-model Spitfire, which was fitted with a more powerful Rolls Royce engine that required a four bladed propeller. (I wondered how quickly I could foul one of those up!). They still had not engaged in combat but were practicing flying with belly tanks (like we did in New Hampshire with the P39s). This indicated something was up.

Lt. Thibedeau also told me he was so impressed with the new planes, he put in a request to rejoin the 52nd and asked me to join him. I tentatively said I would and made plans to do that. But only a couple of days later, I learned one of my former classmates, when attempting a take-off in his new plane with a belly tank attached, unexpectedly veered off the runway and ended up in a fiery death, when his plane smacked into a massive concrete revetment used for aligning the planes' machine guns. That decided me. I was staying right where I was. That accident created doubt in my mind as to whether the Spitfire's quality and maintenance problems had been whipped. Having said that, I feel confident that had the 52nd been given any of the new American fighter planes, such as the P-51 or the P-47, or even the P-38, I'd have jumped at the chance to go back.

I later heard that sometime in December 1942, the 52nd took off from England and flew non-stop to their new base in North Africa. The word I heard later was that the 52nd distinguished itself admirably in the North Africa campaign and that Lt. Thibedeau had become an ace. They later moved to a base in Italy where they were finally outfitted with American P-51s (Mustangs).

# 8ᵀᴴ Air Force Head- quarters

Immediately after reporting to the 8th Air Force Head-quarters, I was moved around on a string of temporary assignments at several different RAF stations. Most only lasted a week or two. No one told me, but later I noted on my military record these moves were designed to turn me into an expert on how to run a military air base. This expertise was put to use about eighteen months later when the Allies invaded France.

Some assignments did not make much sense to me then, however. I spent a lot of time in the control towers, which would help me later. During this stage, I did more or less whatever the British suggested I do. I was given a variety of tasks at the various bases. Sometimes my job assignment even required me to march with the British units – which was quite interesting! The British have an entirely different method of marching – they swing their arms much more than Americans. Once, I was told off when I didn't swing my arms high enough.

It appeared I was being trained to work in some capacity with the British down the road . . . but that never really materialized. I don't even remember ever being de-briefed by my American commanders on what I learned during these assignments.

At many of the bases I was sent to, I was the only American there. Most British airmen had never seen an American Air Force officer, except what they saw in news-reels or in movies (remember, this was still 1942). Consequently, I was constantly being ogled at and treated like some kind of celebrity. Nice, but sometimes, surprisingly, not so nice. Frankly, I did not know quite how to react to this celebrity status, so I tried hard to remain polite, grateful and military.

At an operational Lancaster bomber base, this fascination the British airmen seemed to have for an American officer's uniform even resulted in my being involved in a very close call, which could have been a serious accident. The Lancaster was a British high-wing bomber, built a little like our B-24. All their sorties (missions) were flown at night. Their jet-black color helped camouflage them. Later, American bombers always attacked in formation, but the British technique remained flying individually, trying to use stealth while the Americans used the brute force of the combined armament of the B-17s or B-24s. The Americans flew day missions as they felt it was better to see the target. At that time, neither British nor American planes were equipped with radar, so finding a target that was dark and unlit, at night, was extremely difficult. The British, however, wanted to keep their casualties down. The British always had their best pilots and bombers lead the way. They would drop incendiary bombs along with the regular payload, which helped light the targets for the following bombers. Even flying at night, the British suffered high losses. The Germans also had radar, which they were able to use with deadly proficiency against these night invasions.

Many comparisons between the British night bombing missions and the American daylight precision bombing techniques have been made by experts, and I would prefer to leave it with them. Nevertheless, I'd like to make it clear the incident I'm describing below occurred in the fall of 1942, or a few months before enough B-17's or B-24's had arrived in England to start daylight bombing missions on a mass scale. At this stage in the war, virtually all bombing and fighter missions were done by the British. We may have been late starters, but we came on strong and finished strong. We also hired a bunch of college professors to do a very in-depth study of the effectiveness of our bombing techniques. You may also read their report. It's on the web. Not surprisingly it's called The U.S. Strategic Bombing Survey Report. I'll tell you more about it later, because I became part of that organization when it was first formed, but I'm getting ahead of myself.

My near miss happened on a day the Lancasters were scheduled to go on a long bombing mission deep into Germany that night. During the daylight hours prior to the flight, I was invited to attend their preflight indoctrination.

Walking up the street with two RAF officers to attend the meeting, I had an unfortunate encounter with an earth-hauling tractor (this type had very large wheels with rubber tires in front and smaller wheels in the rear) immediately after it had entered our street from a side road. As the driver turned onto our street, he suddenly spotted our group, and at the same time, lost control of his vehicle. I tried to jump out of the way but combining his excess speed with my slow reaction time, I got run over. Fortunately, the hopper on the Earth Hauler was empty. Had it been carrying a full load of dirt, I'm sure I'd have been crushed and suffered much more than a dirty uniform and damaged pride. I was able to brush myself off and still made it to the briefing.

The preflight meeting was extremely interesting and was the first British one I had attended. First, one officer went up front and showed aerial photographs of the target and maps of the targeted area and told of the preferred approach for the bombing runs, then showed maps of alternate targets and told how best to destroy them. Another officer showed the preferred routes from England across Europe and to the targeted area, and how best to avoid heavy anti-aircraft fire. He also showed where defending German fighters were known to be based and what to expect from them. Another officer then showed a weather map and detailed what clouds should be expected at different altitudes, plus the direction and speed of the wind at different levels. Finally, the Group Commander got up and summarized the whole project.

The Group Commander, who was very courteous,

presented me with a pair of RAF wool-lined boots (my size too! I still have them in the attic). It gets extremely cold on their high-altitude night flights, so warm uniforms were needed. He also invited me to go along on the raid as a passenger in his lead plane, but I politely declined. I had a good excuse, from the sore back I just discovered I had. (In case you are wondering, the Group Commander made it back. I do not recall how many of their planes failed to return that night, but there were a few).

At another air base, located I don't know where because I had recently been shuttled to several bases and was lost, anyway at this base an entire unit of kilt wearing Scots were stationed there. Understandably in the relaxing moments of the late afternoon these fierce fighting Scots loved to let their hair down and imbibe their national drink. Desiring to be an amicable American guest I naturally joined them. All my family members know I now have my scotch each evening, so for them and everyone else, I would like to inform you it was through this group's spirited and friendly association I learned to drink and like, Scotch whisky. Let me explain what happened and describe just how hospitable these Scots were.

From the time I first arrived in North Ireland to the time I arrived at this base I tried to adapt and learn to like the local beverages, including beer, served at room temperature. That was a very tough thing to do, but since that was the way the natives drank theirs, I and all American servicemen had to adapt or do without. Today, I understand cold drinks are available, but that's little consolation to us WW2 fellows. For a long while, with no ice and lacking any means to have a drink chilled, no alcoholic drink was really appealing or attractive. On the other hand, the British had a much wider variety of beer selections than we had back in America. Just sampling them all took a while. Seemingly their most popular beer at that time was their mild and bitter. I know their pubs sold a lot and I bought my share. But at this particular base most all

the officers ordered some form of Scotch whisky. Naturally. That was to be expected.

I would like to correct here what may be a common misconception about how the Scots drink their
whisky. Or should I say, how this group drank it back in
1942. Of course, I can't speak for all other Scots, but this
group took great pride in having earned the reputation of
being the toughest, fiercest, fighting group in all of Great
Britain, so I think the standard they set would be a fair
measuring stick. What may be surprising -- they don't necessarily all drink it neat. Oh, a few did, but most drank it
with an additive. Several at the bar ordered their scotch
with seltzer, but many more ordered their scotch served
with a 'splash'. That was probably the most popular order.
I tried going native and tried each, finally settling on
scotch and water, which is still my preferred drink. But
now I only ever have one drink. Honest. Well, occasionally
I make an exception and have a second, but as most of my
family will attest, it's rare.

The first evening I was there, being the first and
only American officer on base, I found myself being hus-
tled to the Officers' Club. There I was treated more
hospitably than I'd ever encountered before. Even though
I was sent to their base to observe and learn and held only
the rank of a lowly Second Lt., I was hosted and toasted
more like I was a visiting high-ranking dignitary. Basically,
their Officers' Club was equipped much like all other British Officers' clubs. It had two large pool tables, about a
half dozen card tables, and three or four well used dart-
boards. But on this date, the principal gathering place was
the bar. Included in the group that kept insisting on buying
me drinks, (scotch of course) -- more in fact than my body
was designed to handle -- was one rugged looking, kilt-
wearing Scottish officer. Early in the evening my attention
became irresistibly focused on a knife he was wearing
strapped to the calf of his leg just below the hem of his kilt
that displayed a most gorgeously ornate engraved handle.

Somehow, I resisted making comment until later in the evening. Then along about the third drink, while feeling rather camaraderie like, I became sufficiently emboldened to innocently ask if I could see his knife. Even though I was slightly numbed from three scotch drinks, I was able to detect, and I still vividly remember both the slight hesitation he took and the startled look in his eye, like he was surprised at my request, before he slowly bent over and removed his knife from its sheath. Then, using its razor-sharp point, he pricked his finger, drawing blood. He next handed me the knife the courteous way, handle first. Impressed and mystified I asked. "What in hell was that all about? Why did you do that?" In a soft voice just above a whisper, he answered, "We take an oath that says, when we draw our knife somebody has to bleed". You can be assured I never asked another Scotsman to see his knife, no matter how beautiful it looked, and there were a number of very fancy appearing knives there! Now I ask you, was that not a very considerate and impressive Scottish hospitality gesture I received, or what?

With another million or so American G.I.'s scheduled to come over, do you reckon his scarred fingers and hands survived the war? It's not likely he would ever stop being a hospitable host and gentleman as it was obviously part of his upbringing and character, but I wouldn't be at all surprised to hear he started avoiding bars where Americans were present.

While I was there, as at some of the other bases I visited, I spent a lot of time in their control tower on the theory that the tower operator knew about everything I would need to know about how the British run their airfields and particularly how they used their radar. Later I spent a week at a British underground vector station where I was able to observe how effectively they handled some actual fighter interceptions. I would also witness a few other interceptions that were done as training exercises. However, at this particular station, I was attempting to learn the grass roots stuff.

Something one tower operator said created a memorable impression on me. I can recall the tower operator telling me, in answer to one of my questions, "That radar station over there is called the "Pundit" station, and that other one about two miles out is the 'Occult' station."

Now my earlier impression was being confirmed. Not about the Tower operator knowing his job. I already knew that, but it was the fact that the British always seemed to have a knack for being intellectual, even down to assigning descriptive names to their radar stations. In America the nomenclature on those stations would probably read something like this; Radar station X-930-RY-001 and Radar station Y- 222-YR-100, but here the nomenclature is more graphic. Very likely, I thought at the time, if I went to the HQ building, and looked up the meaning of the stations title in one of their dictionaries, there is a good chance I would find a rational description of what each radar station was responsible for doing. I did, and it did. Don't ask me to detail how the stations worked with the Control Tower and with each other, I don't remember that. I thought I did well just remembering Pundit and Occult.

At the conclusion of my unguided, unstructured RAF tour in December of 1942, I was back at the 8th Air Force Headquarters, in London. That's where another seemingly innocent event changed my life forever.

After spending a couple of weeks at 8th Air Force Headquarters, I decided to seek some entertainment I had seen promoted on our bulletin board. It involved a big ice-skating show at the ice rink in the London suburb of Richmond. It sounded interesting, so I decided to go! I went alone.

The ticket I bought entitled me to sit in a box in the northwest corner of the balcony. When I arrived, there was a middle-aged lady and her young son, who locked to be 12 or 13 years old, already seated there, watching the warmup practice. We introduced ourselves and struck up a friendly casual conversation, while I admired the skating beauties below. One skater, wearing a red dress with clubs, diamonds, hearts and spades in black sewn in the hem (a foreshadowing of her future passion), was most striking and riveted my attention. I even passed on a casual remark to my hostess friend, something like, "Now there's a pretty one."

*My beloved Shirley. The picture above was taken in 1945. Her last name had been Inselberg, but the family changed it to Selby*

Her answer, "That's my oldest daughter," caught me by complete surprise, but I detected a note of pride in her voice. Then she proudly added, "I also have another daughter in the show, she's the one over there in the blue-green dress."

At intermission, both girls came up to the box to visit their mother and I was properly introduced to them. Naturally, I took advantage of the occasion and got the phone number of the girl in the red dress. We were destined to see a lot of each other over the next 2 ½ years . . . and beyond. Her name was Shirley Selby. (Ironically, Shirley also lacked a middle name.)

One evening, after a date at the skating rink, we stopped at a little restaurant in Richmond to have dinner. While we were studying the menu, the proprietor came to our table and whispered that if we would like a steak, he could accommodate us. This got our attention, as steaks during the war in London were virtually impossible to get because of the rationing. We decided to take advantage of the generous offer. He told us it would be hidden under an omelet and to not make it obvious what we were eating.

The steak was absolutely delicious. We devoured it! We were very surprised, of course, at getting the steak because beef was so severely rationed and scarce, no restaurants could obtain any nor were they ever available to the general public. Only the military got what little was available, and it was even scarce there. In fact, I don't recall ever eating any beef at any military installation for the 3½ years I was overseas.

The next morning on the front page of London's biggest newspaper, mixed in among all the war stories, I was shocked to see a little article that said the proprietor of a small restaurant in Richmond (where we ate) was arrested the night before (the night we were there) for selling *horse* meat to his customers! The plain-clothes detective must have been sitting at a nearby table watching, while Shirley and I were enjoying ourselves, in total ignorance of what we were ingesting.

# SOUTHPORT

From mid-July 1943 to May 1944, I held a rather unique job with my office located in Southport, England. Southport is on the Northwest coast of England, just above Liverpool and perhaps 150 to 160 miles below the giant-sized ferry and transport base in Prestwick, Scotland. The Prestwick Air Base was the required entry point for all transport aircraft, as well as replacement fighters and bombers flown in by the American Transport Command (ATC).

Many ATC pilots were civilian, some of whom were women. They were excellent pilots, too. However, the U.S. agreement with England forbade civilian ATC pilots from "taking off" from British soil in a combat plane. So wherever they landed, they had to walk-off and leave it. Their intended destination would always be Prestwick, but because of uncertain weather there, they were often lucky to find a safe landing anywhere.

My office, in addition to working with the 8th Air Force Headquarters, coordinated aircraft movement between the ATC and three repair depots (Langford Lodge in Northern Ireland, plus Warton and Burtonwood, both located in the Liverpool area). Using two squadrons of ferry pilots, the planes brought in by ATC were then redelivered to a destination given by the 8th Air Force Headquarters. Both squadrons belonged to the 27th Ferry and Transport Group. I was assigned to the headquarters of the same group, carrying the title of "Operations Officer." My old friend, Lt. Gabriel, was a frequent contact of mine. He belonged to one of the two squadrons, but he remained in the London area. As I recall, he flew from either Hendon, or Hesston airports, maybe both.

I read somewhere that ATC during the war made over 40,000 landings at Prestwick. What percentage of those were transport planes making cargo deliveries and how many were new deliveries of military planes (fighters and bombers) I don't know. I never kept a record of what I handled. But I signed, accepting delivery from the ATC for an awful lot of planes between July 1943 and May 1944. We had a small staff, me (now a First Lieutenant, having been promoted on May 5th, 1943), a 2nd Lieutenant, and a Sergeant who did the typing and clerical work.

Very few of our American replacement warplanes came into the U.K. completely ready for war. Each bomber and fighter wing had some latitude in prescribing how they wanted their warplanes to be armored. Even each Group commander had strong preferences. Not surprisingly, each took advantage of their options. Consequently, nearly all replacement bombers and fighters arriving from the States had to be ferried by one of our 27th Ferry and Transport unit pilots from Prestwick, or wherever the incoming plane landed, (which sometimes was a wheat field or a cabbage patch), to one of the repair depots such as Warton, Burtonwood, and Langford Lodge. All modifications were made at one of those three depots.

The ATC reported all arrivals to my office. I signed for each plane, acknowledging receipt. We then relayed this information to the Operations Office of the Air Service Command Headquarters, which was a very short relay since my office was located in their HQ building. They, in turn, advised us which Depots could accommodate specific planes. My office then called each of our Squadron operations officers and assigned to each Squadron those planes they agreed they could deliver. We did that daily. As modifications were completed, Service Command advised us, and 8th Air Force HQ, accordingly. After 8th Air Force provided us with an aircraft's new unit assignment, we assigned it to an appropriate Squadron for delivery. Our Squadron pilots were well aware a war was going on and knew the importance of prompt deliveries. Unfortunately, we had a few stretches of inclement English weather when deliveries became affairs of extreme anxiety. We had seasoned experienced pilots, however, and they were good, very good.

Since I have given you a rough idea of the responsibilities of my office, now let me describe its physical makeup, since, as an office, it was a little unusual and not your typical run-of-the-mill setting. I should make it clear while my office was physically located in the Air Service

Command HQ building; my two assistants and I were actually assigned to the 8th AF HQ in London for administration. So technically, my small unit was a tenant at Air Service Command HQ. Actually, that arrangement was not a problem. In fact, I think it was an asset and obviously was set up that way deliberately. We worked together just fine.

A lot of messaging took place in my office, which was a relatively large room, perhaps 20' by 20', with one window and one door. Its most unique feature, however, was that all four walls were entirely covered with blackboards from about 2½' above the floor, all the way to the ceiling. These blackboards were used for entering all key identifying information regarding all new replacement aircraft arrivals. Each blackboard had horizontal lines drawn about 2" apart. With this line spacing, a person sitting at a desk in the center of the room talking on the telephone (such as myself) could easily read and discuss all written entries on any of the blackboards. The aircraft entries remained on the boards until the aircraft were delivered to their final operating unit. At the end of each day we would transcribe every entry from our blackboards onto a very long teletype report (they averaged about 6 ft long), which was sent to several addressees, such as SHAEF, USSTAF, 8th AF HQ, Bomber, Fighter, Troop Carrier, and Air Service Command, to name a few. Usually we were still working at 10:00 PM just getting out the report. Getting very little feedback from those receiving these reports, I often wondered, while working on the report, if all the addressees receiving the report were actually using all the information we were sending them. It occurred to me the Germans would certainly be impressed had they been able to tap our line. Maybe they did, who knows?

Unfortunately, because of the blackboards, the room always appeared dark, in spite of extra lights. The window we had didn't seem to furnish a lot of light, but the view nevertheless made up for it. Facing north overlooking a clean, somewhat sandy, beach, I spent many restful moments admiring that soothing, lovely view. Just across an arm of the Irish Sea, we could see off in the distance, perhaps a little over ten miles away, the Tower of Blackpool, which I was told was a somewhat smaller version of the Eiffel Tower. I was also told Blackpool was a noted vacation spot, one of the favorites of the British. In fact, the Royal Lytham golf course where several British Open golf tournaments have been played, was within five miles of the Blackpool tower. But since I was there before I had learned to play golf and became a golf nut, that bit of real estate did not hold my interest then like it would now. Nevertheless, I sat there at my desk in the middle of the room many times gazing across the water at that Blackpool tower vowing to go visit that town someday when my work slowed. Unhappily, that day never arrived. Even though I was at Southport for several months and it was only thirty miles away by road, I never made it to Blackpool.

I should point out my office only handled single replacement aircraft only. Military planes flown over the Atlantic as a complete unit, such as the 302nd Bomb Group, were flown straight to their assigned base by their own pilots. Unless our 27th Ferry and Transport pilots were involved with a plane's movement in some way, it did not appear on our report.

As previously mentioned, our office had one door, which was almost always open. My desk was perfectly aligned with it. That door coincidentally was directly across the hall from another constantly open door. That other door I faced every day was the entry to Col. Bateman's office, with his desk likewise being in line with both doors. In other words, as both doors were always open, we stared at each other eyeball to eyeball most all day, for months on end. At that time Col. Bateman was the executive officer to Gen. Ott[18], the Commanding General of the Service Command. Later, in Dec 1944, my path would cross with Col. Bateman's path one more time. The second time occurred in France. I'll remind you of it when the time comes.

Since I was only a 1st Lt. at Southport, Col Bateman and I didn't spend a lot of time socializing or buddying around together. The difference in rank and age was too great, but I think there was a certain degree of mutual respect. He struck me as a serious-minded military man with a dry sense of humor and had a mellow side that was occasionally detectable. Surprisingly, he and Gen. Ott seemingly had matching military personalities, with Gen. Ott's countenance being slightly more on the stern side. Keeping the military personalities and protocol involved in mind, perhaps you can appreciate how worried that team had me on one occasion regarding an incident that occurred right there in the HQ building.

It started with a written order issued to all HQ personnel by Gen. Ott when he designated a particular day as "Gas Mask Drill Day". Everyone was to keep their

---

[18] **General Ott – from *Wikipedia*:** General Ott was born in Lockhart, Texas... He received his wing in the US Army Air Corps in 1927. He was chief of maintenance at Duncan Field, which later became Kelley Field, from 1941 to 1942. He was promoted to Brig. General in 1943 and retired in 1946. He received the Army Distinguished Service Medal for his actions in 1945 during WW II. The citation read: "Brigadier Isaac W. Ott, United States Army, was awarded the Army Distinguished service Medal for exceptionally meritorious and distinguished services to the Government of the United States, in a duty of great responsibility during World War II."

gas masks handy in their office that day and to actually put them on and wear them when the alarm sounded. My mask was on my desk OK, but unfortunately the alarm sounded while I was on the phone issuing critical instructions to one of our Squadron Operations Officers. Naturally a phone conversation wasn't possible while wearing a mask, so I hurriedly finished and hung up. Now this is where things became extremely uncomfortable for me, because as I hung up, I realized I was involved with another very critical problem of a different nature. I became acutely aware of the second problem while on the phone. It was an urgent call of nature, and this one was now really pressing. No time to tarry. I had to run for it. So off I went, out the door heading straight up the hall towards the rest room. And who do you think I came face to face with, just as I turned into the hallway? Yep, it was Gen. Ott and Col. Bateman, walking side by side, almost to my office and both wearing those ghoulish looking gas masks! I knew I was in trouble, but I didn't have time to explain why I was ignoring written orders and wasn't wearing my gas mask, nature still urgently urging me on. Furthermore, since they were known tough military men, I wasn't sure they would consider my excuse as valid anyway, so I just saluted and kept jogging.

Apparently, Gen. Ott forgave me, for he continued offering me free lifts to London in his personal C-47. (So I could visit my 8th AF HQ Commanding Officer, naturally). And I took advantage of every opportunity. The fact Shirley Selby also lived in London, was purely coincidental. My interest in getting to London as often as possible was strictly military. You believe that, don't you?

In order for you to have a mental picture of how an office bound American Air Force Officer managed to find a place to sleep at a place like Southport, England in 1943, I think a short explanation is needed. For starters, the Air Service Command HQ building was located in a sprawling one-story building near the beach. No place to bunk down there, and the nearest airbase was Warton some twenty-two miles up the road, around a neck of the Irish Sea towards Blackpool. Not exactly a practical wartime commute. In such situations the Air Force provided a monetary allowance to help pay the extra expense for meals and lodging for living off base. In my case, I received a per diem of eight dollars per day. Higher-ranking officers naturally received a little more. Eight dollars may not sound like much money to you, and at today's prices it isn't. But in those days, it bought quite a lot. A good wholesome meal, for example, could be purchased for fifty cents and a night's lodging in a nice Southport hotel would have cost no more than four to seven dollars. Many officers stayed in a hotel. They enjoyed that life. Personally, I preferred renting a room in an English family's home. It not only saved money but there was the added benefit of being able to fraternize and socialize with the locals in their own home. Most seemed eager to meet Americans and tried to be good hosts to the swelling force of arriving American military men.

At this point it would seem to be an appropriate time for me to do an in-depth profile on my particular hosts there in Southport as any good writer would do, but know what? I can't. The intervening fifty-nine years have taken their toll, and truthfully, I don't recall much about them. I only remember they were nice pleasant people and did their best to make me welcome. I also remember their house was located about four maybe five miles southwest of our Air Service Command HQ. To get home from work all I had to do was drive my jeep down the principal road, or street paralleling the beach a good distance, then cruise approximately a mile past the beautiful Royal Birkdale golf course (another British Open venue) on my left. The drive home in good weather usually took no more than five to seven minutes. With an absolute absence of any other vehicles on the street to compete with, I could drive my jeep at whatever speed I felt was comfortable. Normally that was near wide open, or in my jeep's case, 65 mph. I liked driving fast. It was so inviting, with the streets being open and clear of traffic. Of course, those speeds were achieved only in good weather periods when the visibility was good. Unfortunately, it did get foggy sometimes, particularly during the winter and early spring. In an environment such as we had with a close proximity to an industrial district with its numerous smokestacks belching black smoke, the fog absorbed enough smoke to produce an even thicker fog. There was one particular night I recall quite vividly when the fog was so bad the trip home took more than three hours. It would have taken even longer but I finally wised up, abandoned the jeep, and walked.

It was around 10:00 pm when I left for home, or as soon as we had placed our last report on the military Teletype. Immediately, I learned my headlights were a liability. Instead of providing visibility on what was a very dark night, the light reflection on the fog was so blinding, I elected to turn them off and attempted to navigate home by hugging the left curb and navigate by shining my flashlight downward on the curb. Unfortunately, I could see absolutely nothing in front of the jeep, not even one inch, but it didn't matter, there should never be anything in front of me anyway and I had to drive so slowly in my lowest gear carefully hugging the curb I wouldn't have hurt anything even if I did hit it. Anyway, that was my reasoning.

Unfortunately, the street curb curved a lot, as most English streets do, and not knowing whether each curve was the beginning of an intersection and not being able to see across the street I would have to stop, leave the jeep, this time with its lights on so I could find it again, go across the street to find where to aim my jeep to hit the next correct street (if it was an intersection), then hope I could return to my jeep and navigate dead reckoning style to where I needed to go. Forward progress was slow and tedious but I stubbornly crept onward, when all of a sudden, my jeep jolted to a stop, like it had hit a brick wall. In fact, it had. This particular brick wall ran completely across the street. Now I had a rough idea where I was. There was a rail line running parallel to the street I should have been on, by a distance of a little less than a half-mile. All residential streets running 90° to the rail line, with the exception of main arteries, terminated at the rail line with a brick wall. This effectively prevented anyone such as me from driving across the rail line in front of a train. Now, I made the decision I should have made at the beginning. I abandoned the jeep at the wall and walked the remaining two miles. It was faster and much easier navigating. Thank goodness the flashlight batteries held out! The next morning, with the help of daylight, I was able to recover my jeep, probably without anyone ever knowing it was there. No one could have seen it unless they were right on it, and not many people would be walking down a dead-end street anyway unless they made a wrong turn like I did.

While I was at Southport, I always managed somehow to go to Warton Air Base enough times to get in my monthly minimum four hours flying time. Since flight pay amounted to an extra 50%, the amount was too substantial to ignore. Almost every base had two or three planes of some description - American or British, old training planes, or old combat planes -- available for office bound pilots to use for that purpose. One of my favorites to fly for pure pleasure was the British Tiger Moth. It was a biplane much like our primary trainer, the Stearman. The Tiger Moth however, had a liquid cooled in-line engine as compared to the Stearman's radial engine. The Tiger Moth was a little lighter and smaller than the Stearman and since it had less power, it was also a little slower. Nevertheless, it was a good plane for performing acrobatic drills. When flying the Tiger Moth, there was nothing to create tension, or nervousness, it was just a relaxed fun flying session.

Another British training plane I flew quite often

was the Miles Master. It was a tandem two-seater low wing monoplane -- a much heavier, more powerful plane than the Tiger Moth. I believe it was their advanced trainer and it required an advanced pilot to fly it. It was a tricky plane to fly. I learned that on my first flight. One thing I was taught in flying school and a rule I unfailingly observed was to always do a series of controlled stalls at a safe altitude on the first flight of a plane I'd never flown before. This way a pilot learns how that particular plane feels when it reaches stalling speed. Different planes have a different feel. Most planes either quiver, tremble, shake, or shudder, for some a wing drops, and with some there is a rocking motion. There are a variety of warnings, but I discovered the Miles Master was truly unique. It gave no warning. On my first flight, upon giving it the customary stalling test, the plane just quietly and smoothly started sinking. Suddenly the bottom dropped out, like someone had just cut the cable hooked to a free falling skyscraper elevator. Fortunately, I was able to recover easily.

On such a plane on all landing approaches it behooves a pilot to keep one anxious eye focused on the air speed indicator to make sure you're above stalling speed, while the other is surveying the landing area. I recall later giving another pilot a check ride on the Miles Master. The landing scared the living daylights out of me. He didn't do what I was expecting him to do, nor what I had advised him he should do, and as a result in the final seconds the situation got a little tense and exciting. Everything turned out all right, but it made me appreciate the constant stress flight instructors must go through in their occupation. I decided I would never have made a good one, nor would I ever want their job.

An office-bound pilot, conscientiously doing his job, will normally not encounter a lot of exciting experiences to turn into interesting stories. Nevertheless, I have one more anecdote that happened at Southport I'd like to pass on. Actually, it involves a second-hand observation, but when I saw the movie "Patton" several years ago, I was reminded of it.

One of the ferry pilots stationed at Warton with whom I'd become friendly stopped by my office one day and invited me to go along with him and a couple of buddies to our Depot base at Langford Lodge, North Ireland, specifically to listen to General Patton make a scheduled speech to his troops at a nearby training camp. Being busy, I thanked him for the offer but told him I couldn't go, I had too much work to do. When he returned and told me what a show I had missed, I was sorry I hadn't found some way to make the trip. He said Gen Patton stood on a stage in front of a huge American flag as a backdrop and made a speech to his troops using the most shockingly vulgar, filthiest language he'd ever heard from a high-ranking officer. His troops loved it.

Not long ago, while playing golf with one of my golfing buddies who had served under Gen. Patton in North Africa, I related this story to him. His reply was, "Yeah, they also called him 'Old Blood and Guts', but the way I saw it, it was our blood and his guts".

# HEATHROW

On May 10, 1944, I was relieved of my job assignment at Southport and given a new, more physically active, and for me, an even more interesting job at Heathrow airport. (That date, May 10th, would have much more meaning to me a year later, but I'm getting ahead of myself.) My new job title was "Flying Control Officer" and I was assigned to the Headquarters and Headquarters Squadron of the 302nd Transport Wing Headquarters. At that time I was not aware that the HQ and HQ Sqn. was the only part of the 302nd with personnel assigned to it. I just assumed there was an entire Headquarters unit located somewhere in England but nobody at Heathrow knew any details. Inasmuch as Gen. Kane, Commanding General of the Air Service Command, signed my orders, I looked to him as being my immediate commanding officer.

To put my unit assignment in perspective, you need to know that normally the Air Force structure called for Squadrons to report to a Group Headquarters, Groups reported to Wings, Wings to an Air Command, and an Air Command reported to a numbered Air Force. In this case, since none of the personnel slots for the 302nd Wing

Headquarters unit were filled at that time, nor were they filled (for whatever reason), until two months later, the HQ and HQ Sqn. that was created and loosely put together, was obviously designed to serve as a suitable vanguard. In effect, it represented the Group HQ. It then fell upon the shoulders of the few men who happened to be assigned to core positions in the HQ and HQ Sqn., to successfully launch the 302nd Transport wing on its maiden military operation in France. Details later.

Because personnel belonging to the HQ and HQ of the 302nd Transport group had absolutely no one else to report to but Gen. Kane, a highly unusual situation was created. In this case, it was a First Lieutenant (me), reporting directly to a Brig. General of a step higher structure (an Air Command), with no intervening officers in between. Almost as unusual, we weren't even located at the same base. Effectively, I did my job with no interference and no supervision. Sounds great, doesn't it? Well it was, really. But as they say, all good things must come to an end sometime. But this one didn't end as much as evolve. The duties were similar, only the locations changed. I'll fill in the details when the time comes.

Heathrow was located in a close-in suburb of West London. As a matter of fact, the name Heathrow Airport may sound familiar. It should. Today, it is the closest major airport to London, has the highest volume of any international airfield in the UK, and is one of the busiest airports in the world. When I was running it though, it wasn't the monster airfield it is today. It was just a grass-covered aerodrome (no runways), used mostly for transport and miscellaneous aircraft.

One of the largest personnel groups to benefit from Heathrow's location was a large group of Air Force Officers with a pilot's rating that were working at the London HQ and needed a convenient place to get in their required flying time. We served a fairly large bunch of them. The airfield was located on the north side of a major street roughly two to three miles west of the Hounslow Underground Tube station, or what was then the end of the line for the London subway system (called the Underground or "Tube"). On the south side of that main artery street was another airfield, approximately the same size as Heathrow, which was run by the British and also accommodated mostly miscellaneous aircraft. On both sides of that main street, between the two airfields, were side streets containing rows of houses. In fact, while I was stationed

John Wait

there, I rented an upstairs room from Morris and Molly Hallet, who owned and lived in one of those houses. I made a lot of bicycle trips from the Hallet's house to the Hounslow Tube station on my way into town to meet Shirley Selby, the only girl in all of Europe I dated more than once.

When the war was over, all houses between the two airfields were razed and the space created by joining the two airfields became what is now the giant-sized airport called Heathrow. I can honestly say way back in May and June 1944, I actually ran the Heathrow airport, albeit the original and smaller one.

What does a Flying Control Officer do? Good question! Well, very briefly, it meant I was responsible for the safe movement of all aircraft, on the ground and in the air, in Heathrow's vicinity. At larger bases, comprising a number of squadrons, the job title for doing exactly the same work is called, "Base Operations Officer". About five months later at another larger and busier airfield I was given that title. In both cases the control tower and its tower operator or operators came under my jurisdiction and it was where I spent about half my time. The other half I wandered about the flight line or visited the operations office. But the control tower had the most interesting action, and where some quick decisive decisions often had to be made. I liked that, and that's why I spent so much time there.

During my brief two-month tenure, the most exciting action we had was the time a V-1 Buzz-bomb hit our main gate. The day started out routinely enough, and it was somewhere around midday when I left the control tower to transact some personal business in the Headquarters building. But just as I arrived there, the air raid sirens started wailing. I hurriedly canceled my appointment and headed for the front door to return to the control tower.

Just as I stepped out of the front door of the HQ building, I could hear the very loud noisy motorboat type

118

sound of the buzz-bomb approaching. Glancing up, I could see it clearly, directly overhead at about 1,000 feet of altitude. Just at that exact second, the bomb's motor quit. There was dead silence as the buzz bomb flipped over to its right into an absolute vertical dive. The silence was deafening, but I could clearly see the name "WAIT" in bright neon lights emblazoned on its nose as it came straight down. I dived down against the foundation of the Headquarters building, hoping the building would absorb most of the shock.

There was a loud explosion and I heard shrapnel bits hitting the building, followed by lots of dirt and dust. But as I got up, I discovered (gladly) I was fine. Looking about, I could see the sentry's hut at the main gate, which was a very short distance (maybe eighty yards) away, was gone and a mangled car there was smoking and upside down. (The sentry and two occupants of the car were killed, I later learned). Running toward the main gate to see if I could help, I became aware I was just one of several headed that way, so I stopped and reversed my field after deciding my help would probably be more useful up in the control tower. I knew the tower would be getting a lot of phone calls, and I figured the tower operator would appreciate help and guidance.

Just as I arrived at the tower, a B-17 parked on the flight line below the tower called in and asked for taxi instructions for take-off. The tower operator gave them to him. This puzzled me, not what the tower operator said, but the B-17's request. Before I'd left the tower for the HQ building a few minutes previously, that same B-17 had called in from some distance out and had asked for our landing instructions. He also added he had a number of passengers aboard who had completed enough missions to qualify for some much-needed R&R, and who chose to spend it in London. Curious, I took the mike from the tower operator and said, "B-17 from Heathrow tower, it was our understanding you had some R&R passengers you wanted to drop off, if that is the case, you must taxi to a special location. Would you mind clarifying whether or not you still have the R&R passengers to drop off? Over."

"Heathrow tower from B-17. Yes, we had some passengers to drop off, but on final approach, they witnessed what happened at your main gate. They just took a vote on it and they all agreed they wanted to return to home base and do their R&R there. If it's OK, we'd like to proceed with our takeoff, over." It was and they did.

Briefly, let me describe the V-1 buzz bomb[19]. It was a small guided missile plane with stubby, squared off wings. Its most unique feature was its motor, which looked like an oversized stovepipe stuck to its tail. Even more unique was the loud noise it made. It sounded like a motorboat, but with volume so loud, you could hear it coming for miles. Actually, it was rather terrifying psychologically because you knew it was going to come down somewhere and you knew it had about 2,000 pounds of explosives. You just hoped it would keep on flying and explode over

---

[19] **The V-1 Flying Bomb** (from *Wikepedia*): The V-1 flying bomb – also known ... as the buss bomb, or doodlebug... was an early cruise missile and the only production aircraft to use pulsejet for power.

The V-1 was the first of the so-called "Vengeance weapons" ... designed for the terror bombing of London. It was developed ... in 1938 by the Nazi German Luftwaffe...Because of its limited range, the thousands of V-1 missiles launched into England were fired from launch facilities along the French and Dutch coasts...At peak more than one hundred V-1s a day were fired at southeast England with a total of 9,521...

The British operated an arrangement of air defenses, including anti-aircraft guns and fighter aircraft, to intercept the bombs before they reached their targets...while launch sites and underground V-1 storage depots were targets of strategic bombing.

open country somewhere. Few did.

A V-1 falls onto London. (Image source: WikiCommons.)

I also recall walking through Bushy Park with my steady date, Shirley Selby, one day, when we spotted a bunch of them flying towards us in a group. Shirley was very nonchalant about the whole thing, but I was a little apprehensive because we were far out in the open in a very large park where there was absolutely no shelter. So I watched them like a hawk all the way until they passed us by, then remarked, "well somebody back yonder is going to get it." I think that's about the way everyone treated them.

At the time Shirley was working in an office, as a draftsman. (About a year earlier, she had worked as an ambulance assistant. That is, she rode in the ambulance and helped load people in and take them to the hospitals. This was during the "Battle of Britain").

One rather infamous story that made the rounds (I believe it was in a London newspaper) involved a buzz bomb that narrowly missed hitting a US airbase in England. The airbase happened to be next to a British farm where they grew Brussel Sprouts. The buzz bomb managed to miss the airbase and landed in the field of Brussel

Sprouts where it exploded – to the collective cheers of all the Americans who had come out to watch! You have to realize the cheering was for dietary reasons only. Today, Brussel Sprouts may be considered a delicacy to many, but at that time, Brussel Sprouts were fed to soldiers daily, often twice daily. After a while, Yanks were absolutely sick of them.

It was while at Heathrow I had the experience I described in the Foreword - on D-Day. What I didn't know then was that in about three weeks' time, I would be going in the same direction these planes were traveling, but that I would be doing my work on the ground, doing essentially the same work as I was at Heathrow.

# CHERBOURG

## The Card

On or about the 24th of June 1944, I received a wallet-sized certificate (that I still have). Since it was issued at a critical time and stage shortly after the Allied Invasion on June 6 and was issued in the name of the top American Air Force General in Europe, Lt. Gen. Carl Spaatz[20], it obviously was considered important. The card said: "Headquarters USSTAF...This is to certify that with effect from 1st Lt. John *R*. Wait having successful-

---

[20] **General Car Spattz (from *Wikipedia*):** Carl Andrew Soaatz (born "Spatz" – June 26, 1891, died July 14, 1974), nicknamed "Tooey," was an American World War II general. As commander of Strategic Air Forces in Europe in 1944, he successfully pressed for the bombing of the enemy's oil production facilities as a priority over other targets. He became Chief of Staff of the newly formed Air Force in 1947.

ly completed training as a flying control officer is competent to conduct solo watches without supervision. By
command of Lieutenant General Carl Spaatz." It bore the
signature of Alfred M Maxwell, Colonel, Air Corps Direc-
tor of Operations. Note that it gave me a middle initial of
"R".

Frankly, I'm finding it to be rather difficult to
come up with a good logical explanation for its existence.
I'll try but lacking all the facts (like what was really going
through Lt. Gen Carl Spaatz's mind), you'll have to accept
a liberal amount of hypothesizing on my part. First, I'm
going to give you a few facts that add to the puzzlement,
then a few theories that might make sense, and then I'll
attempt an explanation.

First, the statement "having successfully completed training as a flying control officer" is puzzling. There are only two occasions in my overseas tour of duty that could even remotely be considered as being a training period to be a Flying Control Officer, and in neither case was I aware I was being trained. You be the judge. The first occasion occurred during the Oct. – Nov. 1942 period when I was visiting RAF bases per 8th Air Force orders. At that time, I was trying to learn how the British ran their bases, and in the process, I learned how to drink Scotch whisky from the Scots themselves, learned the British had such things as Pundit and Occult radar stations, and was even invited to go along on a British night bombing mission. Yet, no one ever told me that in the process, I was being trained to be a Flying Control Officer, nor did I receive any form of certificate at the end saying I had successfully completed the course. Correction! If this wallet sized card dated 22 June 44, was it, then I just got it about a year and a half late, that's all.

The second occasion occurred during that period starting May 10th, 1944 when I was given duty orders assigning me to be the Flying Control Officer of the Heathrow Airfield. Even there, my immediate commanding officer was a Brig. General and he was located at another base several miles away. There was no one at Heathrow that could have been considered a trainer. In fact, I was doing most of the training. As a pilot I knew what needed to be done and did it.

Next puzzler involves why I even needed the card? Nobody else in the Air Force had similar type cards that I knew of and definitely none of my control tower operators carried wallet sized cards. Neither did pilots carry cards, or navigators, or radio operators. In fact, the card I received was the first like it I'd ever seen. The certificates of completion I received from the flying schools were too large for a wallet. So why was I sent one?

And finally, why was such a big fish's signature required? Carl Spaatz was a 3-star General, the top Air Force officer in Europe. Normally such high-ranking officers are never involved in such trivial matters as certifying graduates of a training program. The signature of a much lesser officer would normally have sufficed. For example, when I graduated from Primary Flying School, **Captain** Robert L. Scott certified that I had successfully completed the course. From Basic, **Captain** Lester S. Harris did the honor, and when I made 2'nd Lt. after graduating from Advanced, it was **Colonel** Ennis C. Whitehead, Base Commander who made it official. Well, you get the idea.

At first, the phrase, "is competent to conduct solo watches without supervision," only increased my puzzlement. I thought I already had that authority. I was a pilot, wearing wings of silver. And I had been doing the job for two months without supervision already.

I couldn't imagine anyone in the military questioning my competence to conduct a solo watch, and at Heathrow no one challenged me. In fact, when I had the mike and the situation was a little sticky, I often made it a point to let the other pilot know he was talking to someone who had been there and understood his problem. I always considered it a confidence builder. Furthermore, when Brig. Gen. Kane issued orders on May 10, assigning me to the HQ and HQ Sqn. of the 302nd Transport Wing with the job responsibility of being the Flying Control Officer at the Heathrow airfield, I assumed conducting solo watches just automatically went with the job, so I did it. A Tower operator must be given some relief. It is a stressful job and he'd go nuts otherwise, plus he needed a coffee break, a luncheon break, and a bathroom break. Therefore after turning it over and over in my mind for a period of time I finally concluded there must be a more subtle and obscure purpose behind this card than its contents state.

As a matter of fact, the more I studied it, the more I became convinced the phrase "By Command Of Lieutenant General Carl Spaatz" contained the card's most significant words. For some reason, those words seem to be saying that something was up, at least something more than bestowing a routine certificate on a bewildered graduate. Like maybe the top man is watching. But right at that moment I couldn't understand why.

Let me compose an imaginary scenario that hopefully will explain all the above puzzling facts. No guarantees, because this may or may not be true. Frankly, I really don't know the truth, but this scenario fits. Let's assume sometime in the Spring when the Air Force's invasion plans were being worked on, Brig. Gen. Kane, (or his predecessor, Gen. Ott) began a detailed review and study of all his office-working pilots in an effort to maximize the utilization of their training and talents. Perhaps he spotted something in my records that could, by a little devious military manipulation, reclassify that Oct-Nov. '42 period on my record, into a Flying Control Officer training period. Perhaps he even got Lt. Gen. Carl Spaatz to approve it. Or, it may have even been the other way around. Who Knows? Or, I might be on the wrong track entirely.

Nevertheless, little things went through my mind such as, well they must be conducting planning meetings at the top level and maybe they have slotted a spot for me. Maybe it even has something to do with the invasion? Here's how the logic developed. A massive storm struck the English Channel for the three days of June 19, 20, and the 21st. It wrecked scores of landing craft and smashed our artificial harbors (called Mulberrys). Our only American Mulberry was damaged beyond repair. This put an enormous pressure on our Navy to stay on schedule in delivering war material and supplies to the invading armies. Now it was time for the Air Force to step forward and help out. It was also where I fulfilled the duty the wallet-sized card said I was trained to do.

In just a little over two weeks after receiving the wallet-sized card, I learned the date on the card was more than just incidental happenstance. I was on the continent doing my thing as a Flying Control Officer in the most rustic, primitive conditions I could imagine, while having to handle a surprisingly large volume of airplanes.

## Querqueville

On or about July 1st, Maj. Kelly (not his real name, which I have, unfortunately, forgotten) and I were walking around visually inspecting a grass-covered field adjoining the west side of the Cherbourg[21] harbor, near

———————————

[21] **The Battle of Cherbourg (*Wikepedia*):** The Battle of Cherbourg was part of the Battle of Normandy during World War II. It was fought immediately after the successful allied landings on June 6, 1944. Allied troops, mainly American, isolated and captured the fortified port, which was considered vital to the campaign in Western Europe. It was a hard fought, month-long campaign.

On June 18th, the US 9th Infantry Division reached the west coast of the peninsula, isolating the Cherbourg garrison from any potential reinforcements…There was little opposition on the western side of the peninsula and on the eastern side, the exhausted defenders around Montebourg collapsed. Several caches of V-1 flying bombs were discovered … in addition to a V-2 installation at Brix.

In two days, the American divisions were withing striking distance of Cherbourg…launched a general assault on June 22. Resistance was stiff at first but the Americans slowly cleared the Germans from their bunkers and concrete pillboxes. Allied naval ships bombarded fortifications near the city on June 25th. On June 26h, …British elite forces launched an assault on Octeville….The harbor and and the arsenal surrendered on June 29th, after a ruse by Allied officers, Capt. Blazzard and Col. Teague, convinced the German officers to surrender the peninsula, bluffing about their manpower and ordinance. Some German troops cut off outside the defences held out until July 1st.

the town of Querqueville.

    While I kept no diary, I am quite confident of the July 1st date, because I can recall thinking just three days later: 'it was exactly two years ago I was celebrating our Independence Day holiday on the high seas aboard the "Duchess of Bedford" troopship in a convoy navigating a course across the Atlantic immediately behind the Battleship *Texas*.[22] The next year, I was at Southport, England. Now here I am celebrating our Independence Day holiday in France watching the same *Texas* and the Battleship *Ar-*

---

[22] From *Wikipedia*: The *USS Texas* (BB-35), is a New York-class battleship. The ship was launched on 18 May 1912 and commissioned on 12 March 1914.

    Soon after her commissioning, Texas saw action in Mexican waters following the "Tampico Incident" and made numerous sorties into the North Sea during World War I. When the United States formally entered World War II in 1941, Texas escorted war convoys across the Atlantic and later shelled Axis-held beaches for the North African campaign and the Normandy Landings before being transferred to the Pacific Theater late in 1944 to provide naval gunfire support during the Battles of Iwo Jima and Okinawa. Texas was decommissioned in 1948, having earned a total of five battle stars for service in World War II, and is now a museum ship near Houston, Texas. [It] became the first US battleship to mount anti-aircraft guns, the first US ship to control gunfire with directors and range-keepers (analog forerunners of today's computers), the first US battleship to launch an aircraft, from a platform on Turret 2, and was one of the first to receive the CXAM-1 version of CXAM production radar in the US Navy.

    Among the world's remaining battleships, Texas is notable for being the first US battleship to become a permanent museum ship, the first battleship declared to be a US National Historic Landmark, and is the only remaining World War I–era dreadnought battleship.

*kansas* bombard German gun emplacements embedded in the hills just above our air base. It was a spectacular show; one I'll never forget. Wonder where I will be on Independence Day, next year?' Well at that time I obviously had no idea, but I'll give you readers a sneak preview. I'll be married and living in an apartment in London. A lot happened in the interim.

The harbor appeared small. I assumed the size of the harbor was the reason it was not being used, but I learned later the Germans had mined it before leaving. However, the sod field adjoining it had been used as Cherbourg's municipal airport, even though it was too small.

Maj. Kelly and I had been given the job of making the field operational for C-47 aircraft. Apparently, because of the severe storm on June 19, 20 and 21, the Navy was encountering unexpected problems in transporting much needed invasion supplies, and the Air Force had been assigned the job of helping out on an emergency basis.

Maj. Kelly was to be the Base Commander, and I was the Flying Control Officer (same job as at Heathrow). Technically, I did not report to Maj. Kelly, the Base Commander, even though he outranked me. We were both components of the Headquarters, and Headquarters Squadron of the 302nd Transport Wing. As such, we both reported directly to Gen. C.P Kane, the Commanding General of the Air Service Command, of which the 302nd belonged. I liked Maj. Kelly (and I think he liked me). We got along very well. I relied on him very strongly for advice and counseling. This relationship was particularly helpful in a sticky situation, which I will tell you about shortly.

Because time was critical, the inspection was brief, but thorough, for the time allowed. Maj. Kelly, being responsible for providing food, shelter, and health facilities for present and future base occupants, was notably interested in inspecting a few small vacant buildings that could be cleaned up for living quarters, and another for a kitchen and dining facilities. Sewage seemed to be a question mark, so Maj. Kelly had a deep trench dug. After a tent was put over it, that became our latrine. The landing field, though smaller than we'd like for a military airfield, was deemed safe and usable. C-47s are capable of landing safely in a comparatively short area.

My biggest problem, and the problem for the unloading engineering officer, consisted of inadequate parking space for the planes where they can be unloaded, particularly as a large number of planes were expected. Between the airfield and the beach to the south was a fairly large vacant field (I'm guessing 50 acres) that would have been a great parking area. Unfortunately, it was off limits. All over it were German warning signs that said "MINEN" in large red letters. To my knowledge, it was never tested to see if it really was mined. I certainly had no desire to test it personally. Nevertheless, I entered a request to have the field cleared, because I needed the parking space, but my request must have had a low priority because when I left 2 $\frac{1}{2}$ months later, the signs were still there.[23]

In the afternoon, I met the men who were to compose my crew. Second Lieutenant Paul Wolfe (not his real name) was to be my Control Tower Operator, which was a little misleading, as we had no control tower. Then there were three enlisted men. As I recall, there was a Sergeant,

---

[23] According to *Wikipedia*, the minefield was cleared of 4,500 mines in September. This was not an easy job as most of the mines did not register on the mine detectors. This meant an extraordinary effort was required and resulted in the awarding of several Bronze Stars. The airfield no longer exists, as a naval academy and suburb have been built on the site.

a Corporal, and a Private. The Corporal and the Private were radio experts. However, beyond their basic duties of ensuring our radio equipment always worked, they also did a lot of field work like putting up signs, flags, etc.

*Pictured above is the C-47, nicknamed "Gooney Bird". The civilian version was the workhorse DC-3. I did not realize it at the time, just how familiar I was to become with the Gooney Bird.*

## The "Show"

The biggest problem facing us was the lack of a Control Tower. We explored but could not locate anything in a suitable location that could be utilized as a substitute for a Control Tower. Consequently, our tower operator had to issue his landing and taxiing instructions while standing on the ground. Not a preferred arrangement, but since the first wave of planes were due at the crack of dawn the next morning, there was no other choice.

Right on schedule, an entire squadron of C-47s showed up at the crack of dawn, requesting landing instructions. Then the floor show began.

I don't know where Lt. Wolfe received his training, or who could have recommended him for this particular job, but he was obviously a misfit. He performed like he was a star nightclub master of ceremonies -- laughing, telling jokes, talking to the pilots like they were long lost buddies. Obviously, he was more excited than anybody in France, and he showed it. Only what he was doing was not only against good procedure, it was dangerous.

I finally took the mike from him and told him, "This is the way I want you to do it." Then I kept the mike and directed traffic for the next half hour, trying to keep my conversation crisp, but calm sounding, and most of all, brief. Then I turned the mike over to the Sergeant briefly, while I took Lt. Wolfe to one side for a little lecture.

I explained to the Lieutenant: "For three years I've been in the Air Force, as a pilot and an Air Cadet, and during that time, I must have participated in, or listened to a few thousand Control Tower transmissions. And I will state categorically the style you are using here is one I've never ever heard before. Furthermore, I hope I never hear it again!

"Lt. Wolfe, I don't know if you picked up that style at your last base, or if they approved your using it, which I doubt, I only know you are not welcome to use it here. I also know you were never taught that style at any training school. Not only do I not like it, it's bad Control Tower communications form, and it can even be dangerous.

"Look at what's happening. We've got planes lined up wanting to take off, but they can't for two reasons: (1) They can't get on the radio to get permission because of your lengthy monologue and, (2) there is a constant stream of planes in the landing pattern who are now landing without permission because they couldn't break into your monologue either.

"Let me explain a few things to you. There is a time and place for good humor and levity, but this is not one of them. You might be surprised to learn not all the pilots out there are even amused or are particularly enjoying all those jokes. Most, if not all, take their flying jobs very seriously, and since this is not exactly a joy ride, they are on, most are not in a very jolly mood anyway. Some may even be in a nervous state for they know they are in a war zone and they know bullets are flying about not too far from here. For those pilots in a tense or worrisome mode you need a very calm voice, and your delivery is about as near the exact opposite as you can get. All the pilots have been briefed that Germans are still in the underground tunnels in those hills above us, and, while the big German guns may have been temporarily silenced by previous Naval gunfire, I'm sure its crossed some pilots minds that it's possible the Germans might get one or two of those big guns working again. But probably the thought that causes the most concern is the long shot possibility that German fighters might suddenly appear from beyond those hills. If there is any plane in the world that would make a good sitting duck target, it's a C-47, and those pilots know it, believe me.

"Then too, because you are hogging so much of the airtime, a pilot sighting a bogie or wanting to report an emergency of any kind is going to have a tough time getting on the air to report it. In addition to what I've just said there is another very good reason to cut your out of place good humor monologue, and I'm sure this has never crossed your mind either. There are a few wild as March hare pilots flying around out there listening, who may interpret your exuberant attitude as being a good excuse to put on an equally wild aerial show. I'm talking about stunt flying a C-47 across the field or approaching the field and landing with both engines shut down, or doing some other wild, stupid stunt, as in, top that! Funny fellow! Don't laugh. Just don't think it can't happen, because it already has at other fields, and with a lot less encouragement than you're giving them.

"Lieutenant, when a pilot calls in for landing instructions, you know what you are supposed to tell them. Somewhere in your past you have been trained to simply give them the wind direction and wind speed, the direction they are to land, their position in the landing pattern, and their altimeter setting. Then sign off, shut up, and listen. That's what I want you to do here. Be professional. Remember, to promote calmness, you have to be calm. And above all else, be brief!

"OK Lt. Wolfe, I've given you several good reasons why you should change your delivery, now get back out there and take over from the Sergeant and do your work properly! That's an order! "

I don't think Lt. Wolfe heard a word I said. He resumed his dialog just like my conversation with him had been a temporary interruption only. Frustrated, and not knowing just how best to handle the situation, I hopped in my jeep and raced off to the other side of the airfield where several planes were being unloaded while some were wanting to leave but couldn't. We had a giant-sized traffic jam there (a mess, in other words) and I thought perhaps some personal, on-site, hand signaling could help get those big planes moving again.

After about an hour's work, we finally got the worst of the jam over. The problem was, we simply had too many planes for the space we had. More planes were waiting to land before we could get the ones on the ground unloaded and into take-off position. Then, Maj. Kelly came by and offered some words of sympathy. In our conversation, I told him of the frustration I was experiencing with Lt. Wolfe. His response was when he first met Lt. Wolfe, he figured him for a dumb, 'smart-ass' right off. He added, "This project is too important to put up with a fellow that's emotionally immature and had not been properly trained for the job.

"My suggestion would be for you to write the Commanding General, explain your problem, and ask him to recall Lt. Wolfe and send you a replacement."

What he said made sense. As a matter of fact, I had thought about doing just what he suggested, but having never done anything that drastic before, I was very reluctant to take such strong action. Doing so meant one of us would definitely get hurt. But the more I thought about it, the more I realized I had to do what Maj. Kelly suggested. If I allowed this problem to fester, it would only get worse and it would affect the overall success of this operation, and my reputation with it.

As there were no typewriters on this field with which to write a formal military letter, the best I could come up with was to use my personal stationary I used when writing home. Thus, as carefully and factually as I could make it, I addressed my handwritten letter to General Kane, outlining Lt. Wolfe's deficiencies as I saw them, including the complaints I had received from the three enlisted men who objected to the demeaning way he spoke to them. I even included word for word one of the long-winded dirty stories he told over the air as an example of his Control Tower oratory. (As I recall, it was a story about a traveling salesman and a farmer's daughter). Then I finished my letter thusly: (I remember this part distinctly) "General Kane, if you will recall Lt. Paul Wolfe and replace him with an officer who will follow instructions and obey orders, I hereby give you my word that you will see this airfield operated in such a manner that not only you, but the entire US Army Air Force can visit with pride." Signed, John Wait, Jr. 1st Lieutenant. HQ and HQ Squadron 302nd Transport Wing.

I put the letter in a sealed envelope addressed to Gen. C.P. Kane and gave it to a pilot ready for take-off for home base with instructions to hand deliver it to Gen. Kane's Executive Officer. Since it took less than an hour for these planes to reach home base in England, Gen. Kane's Executive Officer had it rather promptly. Fortunately, the General was in and as soon as he read my letter, he told the Executive Officer to issue orders for Lt. Wolfe to report to him immediately. Lt. Wolfe did just that.

What happened at 302nd Transport Wing HQ (in this case, it was also Air Transport Command HQ, as

General Kane headed both) is secondhand information, since I wasn't there. The information I got from Maj. Kelly, who got it from Gen. Kane's Executive Officer a few days later, will have to suffice, but the story sounded good to me.

Apparently, when Lt. Wolfe checked in, he was immediately ushered into the General's office, who then handed him my letter, which was on his desk, and asked for Lt. Wolfe's comments. Lt. Wolfe spent some time reading and rereading the letter (like he didn't believe it), then started addressing his true feelings about me. Apparently, he didn't like me. "Lt. Wait is a goddamn liar," he exclaimed. He then went on to say he never told that joke on the air as I'd quoted him as saying or any of that other 'goddamned stuff.'

Gen. Kane then asked him, "Does C-47 H677 mean anything to you? To save you the embarrassment, let me tell you I personally led a flight this morning, in C-47 H677. I thought it a good idea to get a feel for how well this operation was going to work and judge for myself just what might be needed to improve it. The joke Lt. Wait quotes in his letter is word-for-word what you told me on the air this morning. I was appalled. I knew we had a problem. Now I understand, and I am so glad I learned the true source of the problem.

"Lt. Wolfe, my Executive Officer will help you catch a plane going back to Cherbourg. Get your personal effects together there, and when you return with them, we'll have a new assignment for you."

That, of course, was second-hand information. Now I'm going to give you some unforgettable first-hand information. I almost slugged a fellow officer, which can be a court-martial offense.

Around midnight, while sleeping in the third bunk from the front door of our one and only officer's quarters (barracks), I slowly became aware from a deep sleep, that someone was standing in the front doorway and was shouting in a very loud voice some very familiar phrases. He was quoting from my letter, word-for-word at the top of his lungs to the entire barracks. Was he mocking me? What for? What did he hope to gain? (There were probably eight officers there at the time). I lay in my bed, pretending to be asleep for a moment, because the fellow was obviously dead drunk from the way he was slurring his words, and I was hoping he would run out of steam and just fade away. Didn't work. He continued bellowing louder and louder, again and again quoting my letter exactly. Five fellows got up and were trying to calm him down, including Maj. Kelly, who was in the first bunk. Didn't work. So, I decided it was time to get up and confront the guy. If he wanted physical action, which I was convinced he did, I was ready to give it to him. Even though he stood six feet tall, and weighed 210 or more pounds, and I weighted exactly 142 pounds and stood 5'7 ½" tall. I, nevertheless, was convinced I would be more than a match for him. Not only was I in good physical shape, but I was also very quick, which I knew he couldn't match in his current drunken state.

We stood there toe to toe trading insults, when after a while, I decided I'd had enough. It was time to shut this guy up for good, by physical force, if necessary. So I took a mighty swing right at the middle of his nose.

The blow never landed. Someone behind me, or to the side of me, anticipated the blow and caught my arm. Maj. Kelly, who had moved behind Lt. Wolfe, then put a half-nelson (or some wrestling hold) on Lt. Wolfe, and with another officer's help, dragged him outside and dropped him on the grass.

Strangely enough, that was it. Everything became very quiet then. There was little conversation. Lt. Wolfe departed from the scene. Where he slept, no one knows. As a matter for fact, no had seen him previously all evening. No one even knew he was on base. The last plane had landed at dusk, about 8:30 pm. No one knew whether or not he was on it. But if he was, where did he spend his time from then till midnight? An unsolved mystery! (Apparently, he found a bar, or other source of liquor).

I was to see Lt. Wolfe one last time, roughly a year later. I'll describe the brief meeting later when I get to it. But talk about a fellow being banished to Siberia, or to a Hell Hole, he was! He couldn't have landed in a better spot from my point of view.

## *Texas* two-step

The next morning in the first wave of planes, was 2nd Lt. Barnett, Lt. Wolfe's replacement. He was a nice fellow, and Lt. Wolfe's exact opposite. We got along just fine, and, in fact, worked well together for the next six months.

Lt. Barnett's arrival was to be the only exciting thing that happened that day, which when compared to all the excitement of the previous two days, made the day appear rather drab and dull by comparison. But there's always tomorrow, and the next day was no disappointment. It put on a real entertaining show.

Pre-planned, to insure there would be no unfortunate accidents, like a flying plane meeting up with a flying shell, the show didn't start until the initial wave of incoming C-47's had all landed and all others were prohibited from entering the area. Very shortly thereafter we all heard a series of whistling, moaning, groaning, type sounds followed by booming sounds, resembling bombs or shells exploding. Looking around we could see out in the English Channel, perhaps two miles, more or less, two very large naval vessels firing away. Someone said they were battleships, but since he was no more of a naval expert than anyone else, his opinion might be considered suspect. However, since I had spent a little over a week, two years previously crossing the Atlantic in a convoy, directly behind the Battleship *Texas*, and one of these ships looked like an identical copy, I agreed with him. That made it official. They were battleships. The other battleship we learned later was the *Arkansas*. These were the same two ships that gave these and other German guns such a hammering on June 25th. (*At the time, I certainly had no idea how important Texas would be in my life. I would spend 40 years of my life there.*)

There is no question but what the guns on these ships were big, and I do mean big. When they fired, the black smoke completely obliterated the view of the whole ship. The guns were also big enough they fired shells so large an airman in our group excitedly yelled, "I see 'em! I see 'em! There they go!"

"You can't see those 14-inch shells flying overhead, you dumbbell." I stated. "What do you take us for?"

"Oh yes, I can! Now watch," he replied. "As soon as you see the black smoke from the guns, look straight up overhead and you'll see a whole flock of them, flying really fast, going straight for the target!"

For volley, after volley, after volley, I watched the black smoke from the naval ships guns then looked straight up and saw a lot of sky. That's all, nothing but sky. The flying shells simply weren't visible for me, and according to my annual pilot's physical tests, I had an excellent pair of eyes too. I was frustrated, but I never doubted that the airman claiming he could see those shells, really saw them. The excitement in his voice was too genuine.

One thing I can attest to about those shells is the sound. Standing there on our airfield, watching and listening, was much like watching a war movie in a theater. The sound effects seemed as real as the theater's, and not much louder, well maybe a little bit. In this case, the sound of exploding shells seemed muffled anyway, but the distance to the target (between one and two miles) accounted for that.

What were those ships firing at? Well, a brief historical review involving Cherbourg's capture in WW2 might be of some help. The summary capsuled in the footnote earlier gives much of the story, but I'd like to expound upon that a little as it may help explain the setup. Immediately to the south of our Querqueville Air Base were some very steep hills that were so high they looked like small mountains. Embedded in those hills were three or four large guns the Germans had installed to help guard the airfield and the Cherbourg harbor. The guns were connected by underground tunnels, which obviously provided excellent protection for any troops there. As stated previously, on June 25th our battleships *Texas* and *Arkansas* bombarded these and other gun emplacements in an effort to help our troops capture Cherbourg. These same gun emplacements were also hit by our P-47 fighter-bombers -- More than once. Somewhere along the line these Querqueville guns were hit sufficiently hard to be rendered useless, but the tunnels continued to house a relatively small but unknown number of German soldiers. Unhappily for our frustrated American Generals, the Germans were very slow about coming out and surrendering. So, even though they were not considered a serious threat to our operations, our military high command was determined to get them out of there one way or the other anyway, if for no other reason than that they were the last pocket of Germans in the area that had not already surrendered. Hence a bombardment was ordered. The Germans got the message. They surrendered the next day, or maybe it was later that afternoon. I learned about it the next day. That was when I saw the POWs. It was a fairly long column marching single file up a narrow tree-lined country road, with an armed MP about every 20 yards or so. I do recall their uniforms looked uncharacteristically untidy, like they had been sleeping in them.

A day or two later, out of curiosity a couple of officers and I jeeped up the hills to see just how much damage the shelling had done. We weren't military experts (actually, we were rubbernecking tourists), but the damage was less than we had expected to find from all the fire-works we had witnessed. From our amateur observations, it appeared the German gun emplacements were so solidly constructed, it would have been possible with the right equipment and parts, to repair and have the guns firing again without an extended delay. Of course, these Germans were totally isolated without any chance of getting supplies - or any necessities, such as food and water, and without any chance of rescue, so surrendering was really their only practical choice.

While there, we also took a look at one of the tunnels. The thickness of the concrete impressed us the most. The exposed portion we were able to inspect measured over three feet thick. From all the litter inside that one tunnel, it was apparent soldiers had been living and sleeping there.

## Moonlight Requisition

Early the next morning, I arose to what turned out to be another very busy day, just not quite as stressful. Shortly after sun-up, when the first wave of arrivals had nearly all landed, Pvt. Gregory approached me with a suggestion. He said he had been doing a little exploring, and off in the southeast corner of the field, he had found a number of very long poles. Poles that could be used to hold a control tower at least fifteen feet off the ground. Now all that was needed was a small building to put on the poles and we would have our much-needed elevated control tower. Furthermore, he volunteered, he had done a lot of carpentry work in the past and he felt confident he could build us a tower, if only we could find some lumber. (One thing I'd learned in the past, was to listen to your enlisted men. They often, in their sincere effort to help, come up with good ideas).

Overhearing our conversation, Sgt. Beardsell chipped in with a suggestion of his own, "Why not drive over to Utah Beach (a little over thirty miles southeast of

Cherbourg) and take a look. I've heard there's a lot of junk scattered about over there. You might stumble onto something you can use."

That also sounded like an idea with merit, so I said to the Sergeant "Okay, you are hereby in charge of the control tower. Pvt. Gregory and I will take the jeep over to Utah Beach and see what we can find. We'll be back in about two hours."

The Sarge was right. When we reached Utah Beach, we indeed saw a lot of junk, but after cruising up a narrow road parallel to the beach a fair distance, we were not finding anything that would be usable for our project. Then, after rounding a sharp corner, there it was! A complete building, just exactly what we wanted! It was roughly the size of a jeep. It even had a large Plexiglas picture window.

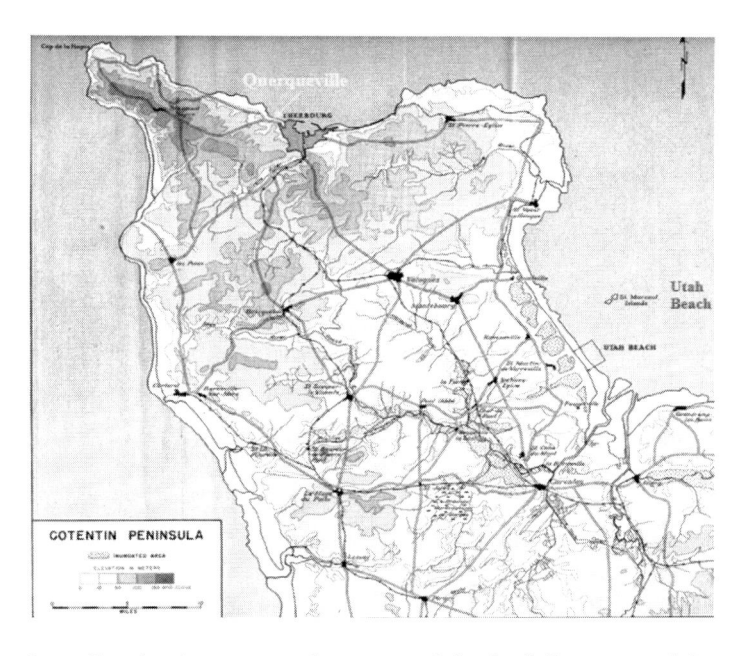

Standing in the corner doorway of the building was a Major, smoking a cigarette. We stopped. I went over to the Major, introduced myself and immediately launched into my pitch. I told him I was from the Cherbourg Air Base, and further explained the severe problems we were encountering handling the heavy air traffic. The biggest problem was that we were operating without a control tower to control the traffic. I then explained what a perfect control tower his building would make. I even used the argument we were flying emergency supplies his units desperately needed to win their battles and we wanted to improve our efficiency.

His reply: "Well Lieutenant, you don't understand, even if I agreed with you, I can't tell you that you can have it. It's not mine to give. This building belongs to Col. Stanley. It's his headquarters building for the XXnd Infantry Division (I really don't recall what Division it was). All his soldiers' personnel records are kept in here. Considering the fact he has a reputation for being a pretty tough soldier, I'd suggest you talk to him personally. If I was to tell you that you could have it, he'd have me court-martialed."

"When will he be back?" I asked.

"Don't know. He was called to a meeting about an hour ago."

"Well, I'm going to return to Cherbourg and get a truck and about four GIs to load this thing. I'll be back at 14:00 sharp. Please, if you see him, explain the urgency of our situation. I would like to get it erected and working this afternoon."

With that, I bid him good day and took off. At Cherbourg, I hunted up Maj. Kelly, told him what I'd found and asked to borrow a truck and four GIs.

We arrived back at the Utah Beach site fifteen minutes prior to 2:00 pm, but no one was there. In fact, no one was in sight anywhere. We even cruised up and down the road parallel to the beach area hoping to find someone to talk to that could tell us what was going on. No one could be seen anywhere. The only thing moving was a few dogs sniffing the debris and a lot of sea gulls. Presumably all the soldiers were in a meeting somewhere. OK, what do I do now? Time's a wasting! No telling when their meeting would be over.

I stared at that little building and made up my mind. I needed that building, and I needed it badly. Definitely, in my opinion, more than the XXnd Infantry Division Colonel needed it. Logic told me that sooner or later, they were going to receive battle plan orders to move inland, if in fact, they weren't getting them now. And, when it happened, they would have to abandon this building anyway. They are supposed to travel light and use tents or live off the land. That convinced me. We're taking it!

"Okay fellows," I said. "Take everything out of the building and pile it up here beside the road and we'll cover it with this tarpaulin. I'll write a note, thanking him for it and attach it to the tarp."

Inside the building was a field phone, a small desk, three wood chairs and several boxes filled with soldiers' records. The men moved the stuff out of the building quickly and we covered it with the tarp. We then loaded the building in the truck and took off.

On the way back to Cherbourg, the enlisted men did little to conceal their enjoyment at seeing their First Lieutenant openly steal the HQ building of a full chicken Colonel right off Utah Beach. (A "chicken" colonel is a full colonel as opposed to a Lt. Colonel).

"No, fellows, that's not stealing," I told them. "That was a standard military moonlight requisition. In battlefield situations when time is too critical to get approval, you do what you have to do to win the war. That's all that counts, and that makes it perfectly legal!" Of course, I had my fingers crossed when I said that.

Back at Cherbourg, everything went smooth as clockwork. Everyone was eager to help. The new control tower was erected and in use before nightfall. An artistic beauty, it wasn't. With its high slanting roof and lower balcony, it looked a lot like my mother's old chicken coop sitting on tall stilts. To us, though, it was beautiful. Now we could see all parts of the airfield, even when a plane stopped in front of us. On the comfort level, the tower operator would now have a roof for protection from the rain, which in the following two weeks, turned out to be fairly often.

Nevertheless, even though I had appeared so confident and nonchalant in front of the enlisted men, I had this nagging worry at the back of my mind. 'What if that Colonel gets so upset when he finds his building missing, that he sends a tank and a couple of armed squads to get it back?' He'd get it, naturally. But do you know what reaction I really got from him? Nothing! Not a word. Oh, who knows? He may have quietly come to Cherbourg, saw his building, and said, "Aw to hell with it. Let them have it, if they want it that bad." Or maybe they did have to move inland. I never found out.

## Army Corps of Engineers

A few days following the Naval bombardment, the Corps of Engineers showed up to install a steel mat runway for us. We needed it. A combination of extremely busy daily traffic and some heavy rains were making the middle of our sod surface airfield a dangerous quagmire. As potholes started forming, we marked them with yellow and red flags, but it was rapidly deteriorating to the point where it was almost impossible for a plane to land or taxi without plowing into a flagged area somewhere. A couple of planes got stuck in the mud and were damaged to the extent they had to be dragged off to a remote area and abandoned since we had no repair facilities.

The Corps of Engineers did the whole project after sundown. Up to that evening, no lights had ever been allowed to be visible anywhere around the airfield as a precaution so the lights would not provide the enemy a target to shoot at. That night, however, our whole airfield was lit up like Las Vegas. Prior to our closing the field down for the day, the Corps of Engineers installed portable lights on eight-foot poles every few feet for the entire length of what was to be our new runway. Portable generators powered the lights. When the sun came up the next morning, the arriving planes had a new steel mat runway that was probably 50 feet wide and perhaps 1,800 feet long to land on (just guessing about the size). I was told in advance they might do the whole thing in one night, but I didn't really believe it. Believe me, when at dawn the next morning, I saw the Corps of Engineers had actually given us a new hard surface runway overnight, I was very, very impressed. Those guys were good!

Let me describe the steel mat. The mats were designed to be interlocking, sort of like the edges of a jigsaw puzzle, but a little more complex. When in place, each mat was approximately 12" x 48" in size and was made from a very heavy gauge steel. To reduce the overall weight, each mat had holes in them, roughly 4" in diameter, spaced about 6" apart. Each mat had to be put in place by hand. That's why I was impressed when the entire project was completed in about 10 hours.

Roughly 10-12 weeks later, I was to witness the Corp's incredible work one more time, at a different location. But since I had already seen what they were capable of doing, they didn't surprise me the second time.

## Busiest Airdrome in the World

After about two weeks or so, things were beginning to settle down into a more customary routine. Maj. Kelly had done a terrific job in making the base a more hospitable place to live. With French cooperation, the sewers had been connected and we now had normal bathroom facilities, even including showers, with hot water! We were also getting more base residents. I was seeing new faces almost daily as new job activities and complete units were moving on base. The base was extremely busy. Our landing strip was described as being the "busiest airdrome in the world," as wave after wave of C-47s ("Gooney Birds") would arrive to offload their much-needed supplies for the advancing allied troops.

Our little base continued to handle an enormous volume of traffic, and grew in size in terms of personnel, as well. In fact, the 31st Transport Group moved their headquarters from Grove in England to our base. However, I had little interaction with them, as I was still a member of the HQ & HQ squadron of the 302nd Transport Group. (The 31st Transport Group, along with the 27th Air Transport Group, were also part of the 302nd).

## Opportunity Knocks

One day, a fairly new fellow, Lt. Steele, indicated he wished to speak with me privately about a very confidential matter. So, we went to the bathroom and closed the door. He said, "I would like to buy the $1,000 you are carrying around in your money belt, and I'll pay you exactly double the guaranteed exchange rate in French Francs."

"What makes you think you know how much I have in my money belt?" I asked.

"Hell, everyone on base knows." He replied.

"How? I've never ever told anyone or showed anyone."

"I don't know. Apparently, someone peeked while you were showering." He said.

He had to be right. It had to have been someone with whom I had entrusted my belt while I showered. I never laid it down anywhere at any time. It was always wrapped around my waist, night and day. And when I showered, I always left it with someone I knew and trusted.

"Steele, there's something fishy here. You aren't offering me double the normal exchange rate just because you think I'm a nice guy. So what gives?"

"I was afraid you wouldn't go for it, but I need

some seed money. Perhaps, you'd float me a loan, then I'll tell you where you can get ten times the pegged exchange rate, exchanging French Francs for either Pounds or Dollars."

"Where?"

"At a bank in downtown Cherbourg."

"You mean a bank will exchange Francs for Pounds or Dollars at ten times the pegged rate?"

"That's right."

"Wow! Is the money real?"

"Looks real to me!"

"OK, we'll work something out. Show me the bank!"

We hopped in my jeep and took off for downtown Cherbourg. When we reached the bank, Lt. Steele said, "We're not supposed to go in through the front door. The bank manager wants us to come in through a rear door and go straight to his office. I'll show you."

Everything Lt. Steele had said was true. The bank manager confirmed he was willing to sell us an unlimited number of French Francs at ten times the allied pegged rate. I was still skeptical. It just didn't seem right to me. But to put it to the acid test, I decided to try one hundred dollars' worth. Now I returned to the airbase with a bulky packet of French Francs. Next stop was to catch a plane, any plane, back to England and exchange the Francs for Pounds. I could do that at our military finance center in London or at any English bank.

Strange as this may sound to readers with more normal human instincts, I was in no great hurry to test it out. I could figure the simple math. Starting with one thousand dollars, all I needed was three round trips at an exchange rate of tenfold to have one million dollars! But at that time, the prospect of garnering one million dollars really didn't excite me all that much. No amount did. I think that's why I was carrying one thousand dollars around in my money belt to begin with. (Remember,

$1,000 was a lot of money then. It was more than enough to buy a nice car, for example). Money didn': mean enough to me to do something sensible with it, like send it home, or put it in a bank. The money I already had was more than I needed considering what little was available to buy at that time in England. For one thing, there was always the uncertainty in the back of all military men's minds as to whether they'll even live long enough to go home. That's one reason poker pots often got so large. Money ceased to have true value. Yes, I did play in a few poker games, won some, lost some. But no real story to tell there!

Another thing, and this may sound a little corny, but I think my patriotic conscience bothered me a little. Somehow, it didn't seem quite right that a noncombatant officer such as me, should be privileged to spend time freely exchanging French Francs for a huge profit, while others only a few dozen miles away, were giving their all. Consequently, it was at least three days or longer, before I crossed the channel to exchange my Francs for Pounds. Actually, even then the money exchange wasn't the primary motivation for me to go to London. My primary incentive was to visit with my girlfriend, Shirley Selby. Financial considerations were a side benefit.

Thinking back on it now, since time makes things look so differently, I'll have to admit, perhaps I was more than just a little bit stupid passing up such a golden opportunity. I, more than anyone on base, yes on either side of the channel, had legitimate reasons and means to make frequent cross Channel trips between Cherbourg and London. The biggest problem might have been with British customs. Bear in mind, every trip from foreign soil to England required Customs clearance on landing, even on military flights. Had I ever showed up at Customs dragging a three bushel sack of French Francs, I'm sure I'd have received a good deal of unwanted personnel attention. The British were faced with a dilemma. On the one hand, they wanted to maximize the war effort, while at the same time, achieving the cooperation of military personnel to observe their Customs laws. They handled it very well, I thought.

At all airbases where planes from the continent were most likely to land, they had a Custom's Department or Counter near the Operation's Department (where pilots checked in). I always checked in with Customs, and I'm sure most military personnel did, but as I recall, it could quite easily have been bypassed.

In the following weeks, I made a number of cross Channel trips from Cherbourg to London, but I never exchanged any more French Francs. I was aware, however, that a lot of others were doing so. In fact, in time, exchanging Francs became sufficiently prevalent, the market price, or rate of exchange, began dropping. But what really put the clamps on the cross-Channel money-changing program came when the London financial institutions unexpectedly placed a fairly low limit on the number of French Francs any individual could exchange. Even so, even after the restrictions and the market drop, there continued to be an impressive number of small-time players. For example, In February, a full seven months later, at Biggin Hill Airport in London, while walking from a plane I had just landed to the Operation's Building to check in, I met a Free French fighter pilot just leaving the building, when a sudden strong gust of wind blew off his cap and French Francs went flying all across the airfield. After helping him retrieve all we could find, I asked him, "What's the market paying now?"

"It's 1.5 times now," he told me. "Not like it was, but you can still make a little money, providing it's not so windy!"

## Fuel for the Fight

While reading our home encyclopedia (*Encyclopedia Americana*), searching for dates, I noted the historian made no mention of our Air Force emergency transport operation. Yet the account did state a large tonnage was brought in through the Cherbourg harbor starting in mid-July. That puzzled me, because our airfield was located right on the harbor's edge and I don't recall ever seeing boats of any size enter or leave that harbor. In fact, I can recall thinking what a shame such a pretty, though small harbor, couldn't in some way be utilized. Apparently, a few boats slipped through when I wasn't looking, and I must admit I was watching the airfield more than the harbor. However, it couldn't have been very busy during July-August-September, or I'd have seen something, I'm convinced of that. (Another account I read on the internet stated that the harbor wasn't fully operational until September which was about the time I left).

Our airfield on the other hand, was like a hyperactive beehive. While the Navy was perhaps bringing in the big bulky (and heavy) stuff like tanks and trucks, we were flying in a lot of critically needed lighter, smaller stuff. Tons of it, in fact. Mostly we flew in quartermaster items such as food, clothing, tents, sleeping gear, ordinary supplies, guns, ammunition, and, yes, we even flew in gasoline for the jeeps, tanks, and trucks in five-gallon Jerry cans. I'm of the opinion General Eisenhower must have felt the items flown in by the Air Transport Operation were critically needed, or he wouldn't have ordered it done on an emergency basis. Yet, the historian gives credit for the several tons the Navy brought in, but the 10,000 tons the Air Force Transport Wing brought in during the first 30 days of their operation at Cherbourg (Querqueville) is not mentioned!

On September 15th, I received a promotion to the rank of Captain, which called for a little celebrating, but since wartime Cherbourg wasn't exactly a place known for revelry, the celebration was very mild.

# Paris

**On to Paris**

The day following my promotion, I received a written order from SHAEF (Eisenhower's Head-quarters, in the heart of London) to report there to a Col. Bjorklund. Col. Bjorklund was a young fellow, much younger than most Colonels. I'd say not much older than I was, but from his immaculate uniform, his demeanor, and precise military bearing, I took him for a West Point graduate. He also had blazing blue eyes that looked straight through you.

He got right to the point. I can recall his speech verbatim. It made a lasting impression.

"Captain Wait, we have a very important mission to send you on, a mission that you haven't been trained for, and we don't have time to train you."

'Wow!' I'm thinking, 'does he want me to be an OSS spy, or something?'

Then the truth: "We want you to take your entire unit from Cherbourg to the airbase of Le Bourget, a Paris suburb, so that gasoline and other critical supplies can be flown in to sustain our Army's progress. You will be traveling through three very active Army Groups, with a lot of bridges out, so travel will be slow. We are allowing you a week to get there, but radio us when you arrive." [24]

"Now there is another matter I particularly want to caution you about, because you fly boys have a reputation for being a little wild, reckless and irresponsible."

He's been watching too many movies, I'm thinking and wondering, 'is he reflecting his superior's viewpoints, Gen. Eisenhower?' Then he continued.

"There is one thing I want you to understand and remember."

Now he's shaking his finger at me!

"A Commanding Officer never eats, or sleeps, until his enlisted men have been fed and provided shelter."

"Yes sir, I can handle that." I replied. "I've always tried to look after them. I've been doing that at Cherbourg, or at least, I thought I was."

"That's what we understand, but I'm reemphasizing it, because it can affect morale and we don't want any letdown or failure from any part of your group. It's that important. Bear in mind, when you arrive at Le Bourget, there will be no units already there to provide hot meals or decent sleeping quarters. In fact, when you arrive, you will be the only Americans there, so you will be entirely on your own for a while.

"Now one thing more. We're giving you some special written orders. Just show them to the M.P.'s at any checkpoint you encounter. They'll recognize them for what they are, and they will give you immediate clearance."

After a little further informal discussion to make sure I fully understood everything, I took leave and headed

---

[24] Editor's note: Paris had been liberated a little over two weeks previous - on August 31, 1944.

straight for the G2 section (Intelligence). On the way there, I peeked at the orders to see if they were signed by General Eisenhower. They were not. The orders said, 'By Order of General Mitchell.' I had never heard of Gen. Mitchell. I wondered if 'Gen. Mitchell' was a code name for Gen. Eisenhower to thwart a few German agents who had been known to flash bogus orders signed by order of Gen. Eisenhower?[25] I never found out, but I did learn from experience the orders I had received impressed everyone I showed them to.

The first people to see them were at the G-2 Section (Military Intelligence), where I asked for and received French road maps. They also gave me aerial bombing maps disclosing which roads and bridges were impassable. With all the material I'd collected, I felt comfortable I was prepared for my 220-mile journey. In fact, I was getting excited.

Back at Cherbourg, I gathered my group together, still the same fellows, a 2nd Lieutenant and three enlisted men, and told them to start packing. We were headed to Paris the next morning. For transportation, we had one jeep and a 6 x 6 truck. The truck was to haul all of our personal baggage and radio equipment for our next control tower. From the quartermaster, I checked out blankets, cots, bedding, tents, and all the miscellaneous paraphernalia I could think of that we might need, plus lots of "C"

---

[25] Editor's Note: I searched the internet and could not find a General Mitchel in the European theater in World War II. However, there was a General William "Billy" Mitchel in World War I who is generally considered the father of the United States Air Force and the namesake of the Mitchel bomber used heavily in WW2. My dad may have been right. They could have used his name as a code for Gen. Eisenhower or more likely Gen. Spaatz.

rations and "K" rations -- Army food.

Early the next morning, we took off for Paris, with Sergeant Beardsell driving the jeep with me riding in the passenger seat with all my maps for navigating. The truck followed with an enlisted man driving and Lieutenant Barnett in the outside, or window, seat. Surprisingly, we made good time, much better than I was advised to expect. There were a few traffic jams, mostly from tanks and trucks, but I tried to avoid them as best I could. Whenever I saw a jam up ahead, I consulted my maps and looked for an alternative route. Sometimes there were none, but often there was. You just had to know where those narrow, winding French roads would take you. That's why I had all those maps.

Around 5:00 pm in the afternoon that same day, we began entering the Northwest Sector of the suburbs of Paris. As we passed what looked to be a Church School containing several buildings, my tired, half-asleep eyes became focused on some shiny aluminum mess kits being held by some American G.I.s lining up in a normal chow line. All of a sudden, Col. Bjorklund's stern admonition 'A Commanding Officer never eats or sleeps . . . ' raced through my mind, and I instantly yelled to the Sergeant driving, "Sarge, pull in here, quick!"

After introducing myself, I showed my orders to the Commanding Officer and asked him if he thought his kitchen would be able to spare enough chow for my group. His reaction was both instantaneous and benevolent.

"Hell yes! Tell them to get their mess kits and get in line, and if you'd like to sleep here, which I'd recommend, tell them they can bunk down in the auditorium over there with my troops. Then in the morning, you can have breakfast with us and resume your trip to Le Bourget, which is just up the street there, maybe 10-12 miles."

We took advantage of his hospitality. The next morning, we arrived at Le Bourget while it was still quite early. We had been given a week to get to Le Bourget, yet we made it in a little over one day. Good thing, too. From the bombed-out mess we found, we needed a lot of time to look the place over and sort out what was salvageable and what was hopeless junk. I knew the Corps of Engineers would be here in a few days, and they would have bulldozers, tractors, trucks, and heavy lifting equipment to fill in the bomb craters and could remove much of the rubble from the demolished administration building. But I wanted time to study the field and try to figure out what would be the best alignment for the steel mat runways. And I needed to determine where would be the best places for parking and unloading the planes. Also, where and how would we construct a control tower?

Le Bourget about the time I took over.

## Le Bourget

Let me describe Le Bourget to you. Briefly, the airfield was quite spacious, especially compared to Cherbourg. But like Cherbourg, it had an all grass surface. As a matter of fact, many European municipal airports at that time had no concrete runways, including the one in Berlin. What little improvement the French made to Le Bourget since Charles Lindbergh landed there in 1927 (in his famous cross-Atlantic solo flight with the *Spirit of St. Louis*), just seventeen years previously, the Allies totally destroyed during their bombing. Not only was the whole field liberally endowed with craters, the administration building was just a pile of twisted girders and rubble. (As seen in the accompanying photo).

After a hasty tour of the field, we determined the best thing to do for our Control Tower, at least to start with, would be to try to rebuild the damaged one from the steel girders and other material from the old Administration building. But before starting on it, we thought we better look over the accommodations on base for a place to sleep.

That is one of the big advantages to being the first arrivals at a new base. We could look everything over and pick the best, most deluxe units, in the best location, for our very own. Everyone coming on base behind us would have to choose from our rejects. Of course, had some General come on base later and said he wanted my quarters, he would have had them instantly. Naturally!

Showing little or no damage from the bombing were several barracks-type buildings that had obviously been occupied by military personnel, first by the French then Germans. We toured them together as a group. Good thing. However, at one very nice unit, which I'd about decided to pick for my own, I was mystified at what appeared to be two toilet stools in the bathroom. One however, couldn't possibly pass a solid BM. Noting my puzzlement, one of my enlisted men, who was much more worldly than his Western Kansas Commanding Officer, explained it was called a 'bidet' and that it was used by the other gender. I couldn't help but blurt out the obvious, 'then what the hell is it doing here in the bachelor Officer's barracks? Our American Officer's Quarters aren't equipped this way. I would guess the French have a more liberal military viewpoint. Maybe our Army ought to take lessons." That got a good horselaugh.

## Corps Comes Through

It was a full week before the Corps of Engineers showed up. By the time they arrived, we already had our Control Tower about 95% finished using nothing but raw muscle, small tools, and a little volunteer help from the French locals.

As before, the Corps of Engineers plunged into the project full blast, accomplishing a surprising amount of work in a short amount of time. Only this time, it was all done in daylight. Another big difference was the use of small bulldozers, which were used to fill the bomb craters. One thing that was not done, however, they did not tamp down the dirt shoved into the craters rock hard. We learned later the hard way that was a big mistake. When we went through a very wet rainy period, the bomb craters became serious hazards. Fully loaded C-47s attempting to taxi across a crater were frequently getting mired down and stuck. A few sank so deep the plane was damaged, which meant pulling the plane to one side and temporarily abandoning it due to the lack of repair facilities.

The Cherbourg operation was obviously an impromptu, rush rush job. No preplanning had been done and we suffered because of it. None of the crew had even met each other previously, let alone worked together, until we met at the airfield at Querqueville. But with Le Bourget, we had more time and a staff that both knew each other well but worked together as a unit. I am very proud of the work we did in getting the field ready much sooner than anticipated by brass.

## Petrol for Patton

At Le Bourget, roughly the same mix of items were flown in as was done at Cherbourg, though the emphasis was definitely towards gasoline. And it seemed to be the same planes coming to Le Bourget as we had coming to Cherbourg. We were right at the heart of the "Petrol for Patton" campaign where gasoline was flown into Le Bourget, then sent on to Gen. Patton's tank divisions There were big stacks of jerry cans, full ones that were just unloaded and empties going back. The gas can was shaped like a book, with a handle all the way across the top. The handle was recessed so that you could stack one can on top of the other. Each could hold five gallons. I can still picture the mountains of jerry cans we had on base. The full cans were loaded onto 6 x 6 trucks, which hauled them off. They returned later with the empties.

*Jerry cans being unloaded from a C-47*
*https://olive-drab.com/od_mvg_jerry_can.php*

Le Bourget became one of the main bases, if not the main allied base, on the continent for supplying our troops. In fact, the 27th Air Transport Group was relocated to Le Bourget, as were several other units.

My status remained virtually unchanged, however, even though on paper I was transferred to a different unit. On October 3rd, the HQ and HQ squadron of the 302nd Transport Wing, to which I had belonged since May 10th, was dissolved and the few officers belonging to it were transferred to other units. We had served our purpose, I guess. What happened to the other officers, such as Maj. Kelly, I do not know, but I was transferred to the 10th Airdrome Squadron, commanded by Maj. Art Kline. It was a paper transfer only. I did exactly the same work and retained the same people in my organization. Then on November 7th, I was given the title of Base Operations Officer. Here again, I did exactly the same work, and had exactly the same responsibilities as I did as the Flying Control Officer. It was just a fancier title, with no pay raise to go with it.

While none of the other changes affected my work or job responsibilities, it did affect whom I reported to. As a member of the HQ and HQ Squadron of the 302nd Transport Wing, which was in a practical sense, the precursor to the whole 302nd Wing HQ itself, I initially reported directly to the top man, General C.P. Kane, of the Air Service Command. That relationship lasted from May 10th, 1944 until early July 1944, when the Wing HQ was officially organized and staffed. At that time, my commanding officer became the Group's first Commanding Officer, Col. Steinmetz. In September, Col. Steinmetz was replaced by Col. L.P. Arnold, who lasted until the first week of December when Col. M.A. Bateman took over. Yep, that's right, the same Colonel who I stared eyeball to eyeball with for several months at Southport. But, like I said, it was no big deal. This time I rarely saw him, and by that time I had a new intervening Commanding Officer in Maj. Kline anyway, who I also rarely saw. In fact, I have no recollection of ever having met the guy, although I'm sure I probably did.

Because of the extra airfield space, or being better organized, whatever, it was so much easier for my group to handle the traffic at Le Bourget than at Cherbourg. As a result, I felt guiltless in taking some time off to do a little sightseeing in downtown Paris. That's where I bought some earrings for Shirley for Christmas (she lost them about two years later in Newport News, Virginia).

A few other American officers could be seen in Paris as well, but there were not many. The lucky ones that were there received very hospitable treatment from the locals. For example: walking along the sidewalk near the Arc De Triomphe, I stopped in front of a portrait photography studio, admiring some of the photos they had in their display window. Most were of Americans and the photos looked great, so I went in. Two of the photos they took of me are now hanging in our hallway. They were obviously done by professionals, and I'm a tough subject to photograph. They not only charged me nothing, they seemed delighted to do it.

Around mid-December (I don't know the exact date), I saw a sight that was truly awesome. It rivaled the sight I witnessed on D-Day, when I saw all those airplanes headed for France. This time it was tanks. Early in the morning, around 7:30, I heard this loud roar, much louder than a C-47. Looking for the source, I saw a tank, followed by a continuous line of other tanks, nose to tail, all headed eastward on the highway that ran by our main gate, at what I assumed was their top speed, or at least their highway cruising speed. Now here's the awesome part. This column of tanks seemed endless. It continued roaring by, non-stop, all day, without the slightest break, until after 4:00 in the afternoon, when we recognized they were probably reaching some stragglers. The last tank went by about 5:30. At one point, using my binoculars from the control tower, I could see the column cresting a hill on the far horizon. They were still single file, nose to tail. Then I did a little mental calculating. If you assumed the column's

average traveling speed was no more than 15 mph, then
the lead tank would have been 150 miles down the highway when the last tank passed our main gate! If there was
an average 50 ft. spread between the nose of one tank to
the nose of the trailing tank, then there had to be over
15,000 tanks passing by our airbase! Of course, I'm just
guessing at the speed and the distance between the tanks –
but I wouldn't be surprised at all to know there were at
least 10,000 tanks passing by that day. I'm here to tell you,
that was one hell of a long string of tanks we saw go by.
Whether or not they were Patton's, I never learned, but we
all assumed they were. One Air Force observer said, "It's
no wonder Patton has so much success. I'll bet he controls
more tanks than the rest of the world combined." To put
this in perspective, geographically, Bastogne, the center-
piece of the Battle of the Bulge, measures exactly 160 air
miles ENE of Le Bourget's main gate.

Another wag said, "Since what we've seen is probably only a fraction of all the American tanks over here,
doesn't it make you marvel at the tremendous job the Navy
has done just hauling all that mass of steel over here? Then
they had to shuttle it again across the English Channel.
Our planes aren't big enough to haul anything like that!"

**Christmas in Paris**
On December 24th, Christmas Eve of 1944, we received a
warning to be on the alert for a possible surprise German
paratroop attack. That night, with my Army 45 Caliber
revolver strapped to my side like an old Western Kansas
cowboy heading out to Dodge City (the only time in my
military career, I ever wore it), I stood on the balcony of
the Control Tower watching the clouds for an enemy
plane. There was a Colonel there, keeping me company,
but I don't recall what his job responsibility was. I can recall becoming very tired about 3:00 am Christmas
morning and telling the Colonel, "I don't think they're
coming. I'm tired. I'm going home to see what Santa left,

then go to bed. I'll let the M.P.s worry about the Germans."

He said, "I agree. I'm going to bed, too " That ended our only military alert. I spent New Year's Eve in Paris . . . but it must not have been too exciting, for I don't remember anything about it. However, about a week later, an exciting break in my military career occurred when I received orders transferring me from Le Bourget back to London.

# US BOMBING SURVEY

**M**y orders said I was to report at once to a Brig. Gen. Sorensen of the US Strategic Bombing Survey (USSBS)[26] in the heart of London. I arrived there early in the morning of the second day, full of curiosity as to what I would have to do with a Strategic Bombing Survey unit (which I had never heard of). I fig-

---

[26] (From the Forward of the report) The United States Strategic Bombing Survey was established by the Secretary of War on November 3rd, 1944. The Table of Organization provided for 300 civilians, 350 officers and 500 enlisted men. The Survey operated from headquarters in London and established forward and regional headquarters in Germany immediately following allied take-over of territory.

It made a close examination and inspection of several hundred German plants, cities and areas, amassed volumes of statistical and documentary material, including top German government documents; and conducted interviews and interrogations of thousands of Germans, including virtually all of the surviving political and military leaders. Germany was scoured for its war records, which were found sometimes, but rarely, in places where they ought to have been; sometimes in safe-deposit vaults, often in private houses, barns, caves; in one occasion, in a hen house and in two occasions, in coffins…

ured the General would fill me in. But when I checked in, a clerk informed me the organization was very new and Gen. Sorensen, himself, wasn't expected to report in for a couple more days. He was flying in from Panama, which was a very long distance away. The clerk then proceeded to fill me in on what the organization was all about and how I was scheduled to fit in. So, for the second time during the war, I found myself as being one of the first people assigned to a major new organization.

In the footnote, I provided text of the foreword to the official USSBS report, filed on the 30th of September 1945, as it describes what went on at the USSBS more accurately than I can. Next, I will give you what I was told the USSBS was all about and what my part in it was to be. Incidentally, you can read the entire USSBS report yourself at xhttp://ibiblio.org/hyperwar/AAF/USSBS-ETO-summary.html.

* * *

The clerk told me the organization was essentially a civilian organization composed primarily of college professors who were recognized experts in their field, be it chemical, metallurgy, oil, electrical power, labor relations, aircraft manufacturing, etc. There were perhaps a total of two to three dozen experts, all of whom could speak and read German. Their duty, established by President Roosevelt, was to analyze the effectiveness of the Allied bombing campaign, and to make recommendations for its improvement. It was felt the military should not be entrusted with the responsibility of critically analyzing its own work. The clerk further said the sole duty of the military part of the organization was to assist the civilians and help them to get the information they wanted. This meant obtaining copies of German production records before the Germans thought to destroy them. The military was to have *one* airplane only, a C-47, equipped with eight seats in the fore part of the cabin and a jeep immediately behind the seats to provide ground transportation when the plane landed. The plane would be making landings as close to the front lines as possible, where dependable local transportation would not be available. The plane had already been modified and delivered. It was now located at the Biggen Hill aerodrome (a former Spitfire base) and available for my inspection. The crew was to consist of me as first pilot (who was first to report), Sgt. Bertolina, from Fayetteville, Arkansas, who served as crew chief, and Captain Geisel, a fellow Kansan from Hutchinson. Capt. Geisel was a trained navigator, but served as the co-pilot, even though he was not a pilot. Although this was not unusual in C-47s to have the co-pilot be a navigator, it did mean that if anything happened to me, there would be no one who could fly the plane. At least Capt. Geisel would know where they were if they crashed. My heart sank as I listened to the clerk tell me this, but I said nothing, as he wasn't the one I should confess my problem to.

## My Problem

Worried about how I was going to handle my problem, I borrowed a USSBS jeep and took off for Biggin Hill. I wanted to see that plane. The trip to Biggin Hill went fairly quickly because, unlike present day times, traffic in London in January 1945 was virtually nonexistent. Because petrol (fuel) was so severely rationed, there were no civilian cars on the streets, only cabs and buses and they were scarce. That meant while cruising the streets of London, braking action was rarely needed. At that time, most people commuted via the Underground (subway) anyway.

When I arrived at Biggin Hill, I found a C-47 plane parked near the Operations building. As I stood in front, looking up at it and realized it was scheduled to be _my_ plane, it looked bigger than all the other C-47s. This one was huge! Maybe that was because I knew I couldn't fly it. That was my problem -- I wasn't qualified! I was a single engine fighter pilot by training. I had never received multi-engine flight training and had never even sat in the pilot's seat of a two-engine plane.

This thought raced through my mind, 'I'll bet there are over 3,000 multi-engine pilots in the European Theater right now who would give their eye teeth and more, to have this job. It would be considered a gem of a job. The thought of living in an apartment in London, with my own jeep, dating my girlfriend, Shirley Selby 3-4 nights a week, answering only to a General, as opposed to living in a barracks on a military base as just another pilot, is enough to make any pilot salivate.

I could come up with two probable explanations as to why I was picked:

1. Some dumb clerk was given the job of handling this as a routine transaction and didn't notice my military record showed an MOS of 1051 (pilot, single engine), or didn't consider it important. To fly C-47's, an MOS of 1054 (pilot, twin engine) is also needed. I might add the military in WW2 was well known for placing square pegs in round holes.

2. An alternate explanation (and the one I liked better) went something like this: Let's assume there was a high-ranking Air Force General who was sufficiently impressed with my job performance at both Cherbourg and Le Bourget that, when this opening suddenly occurred, he thought of me as a good candidate. Furthermore, he must have been confident I could easily fly a C-47, even though all my flying experience had been as a single-engine pilot. (The C-47 is a very stable, easy-to-fly airplane). In other words, rather than sending me to a special base to receive indoctrination training as was normally done, he was giving me the job opportunity, but was leaving it up to me, if I wanted the job, to voluntarily get myself qualified and checked out to fly C-47s. Wow! I liked that idea, and the more I thought about, it, the more it made sense. Now, what I had to do right quick was find someone to give me a

check ride!

I looked at my watch, it wasn't late, only about 10:00 am, plenty of time to drive to a nearby C-47 base, which was less than an hour away, and find someone willing and able and had the time to give me a ride. So, I hopped back in my jeep and took off.

In the Operations building, I got lucky and located a Captain who said he'd had some repair work done on his plane and wanted to take it up for a test flight. He suggested I could come along, and he'd check his plane, and me, out at the same time.

The first thing we did was go up and do a few stalls. This is a great confidence builder, because the pilot learns just how a plane feels and how it responds in a stall situation (different planes have a different feel), and at what air speed to expect one. Following this, he showed me how to feather a prop, and how to trim the plane for single engine flight. Then we shot some landings, several of them, in fact. Enough that I was convinced I'd never have any trouble landing a C-47. Around 4:00 pm, I was on my way back to London confident I could fly that plane and do it well.

Now I had a problem bordering on a dilemma, do I make a confession regarding my total void of C-47 flying experience to Gen. Sorensen[27] when I first meet him, or do

---

[27] **Brigadier General Edgar P Sorensen (from the US Air Force website):** Edgar P. Sorensen was born in Glenville, MN in 1893. He graduated from the University of Washington … in 1915, and in July of that year was commissioned a second lieutenant in the Coast Guard Artillery Corps in the Washington State National Guard. In November 1916, he was promoted to captain, and in December 1917 was appointed captain in the Signal Corps Reserve of the US Army…

In September 1943, he was assigned to the Sixth Air Force in

I just casually start flying with him and those civilian college professors aboard just like I'm an old pro in the transport business doing my normal thing? Something else to consider is the possibility he's been previously informed and already knows? All kinds of wild thoughts like that raced through my mind. But, one by one I rejected them all. Nothing made sense. Normally when a General has been assigned to head up a new organization such as the USSBS and is authorized to have a C-47 and a crew to fly it, he shouldn't be expected to find it necessary to set up a training program for his pilot. That pilot should have arrived not only already checked out and qualified on that plane but experienced as well. I concluded therefore, that my best chance to keep the job, which I wanted very much to do, was to assume he didn't know, and to volunteer nothing. I might blow the whole thing if I did. He might even get sufficiently upset at learning the truth to complain to a higher command, and then I really would have lost it. Consequently, I mentally prepared an answer I could use just in case in my initial interview, Gen. Sorensen should

---

the Caribbean Defense Command, and the following month became chief of Joint Staff, Joint Command Post, in the Panama Canal Department. In May, 1944 he assumed command of the Sixth Air Force.

He returned to the United State in January 1943 for assignment to the USSBS in Washington DC and later went overseas with that organization. In August 1945, he was appointed Chief of the Services Division of the USSBS.

The following month, he returned to the US and was assigned to the office of the Under Secretary of War in Washington….

General Sorensen has been awarded the Bronze Star Medan and is rated Command Pilot, Balloon Pilot, Combat Observer, Aircraft Observer, and Balloon Observer.

pointedly ask me about how many hours flying time I had on a C-47. I would tell him, "I don't know exactly but I've found it to be an easy plane to fly and I've got about a thousand hours in total on a whole variety of planes, a lot of it on P-40s, P-39s, and even some on Spitfires. General, I want this job and I give you my word I can safely fly you and anyone else, anywhere you want to go this side of the German lines." I figured that statement which was truthful and sincerely given ought to impress him sufficiently.

## The Mystery

For the rest of that afternoon and night and continuing to the present day I've wondered, who was my benefactor? Either a colossal error was made, or some military bigwig was intent on rewarding me with a highly desirable flying position, even though it meant risking possible criticism for his actions. Consider this, the 302nd Transport Wing, the organization I had just departed, consisted of two very active Transport Groups, the 31st and the 47th, each of which had approximately 60 pilots with over a thousand hours flying time on C-47's. Any one of the best of those two groups would have been a highly logical choice. Experience, skill, and know-how with C-47s, they all had it, with spades. And this position was unique. I would be the only pilot for a major task force.

Then from the pilot's standpoint, just picture the difference in living conditions that would be encountered between flying for the 302nd and flying for the USSBS. Most 302nd pilots lived in barracks on base and ate in a mess hall, the USSBS pilot was expected to live in a nice London apartment, receive liberal per diem pay, and have his own jeep. Obviously, any one of them would have jumped with joy at a chance to be selected. Yet the guy with orders in his pocket to fly a C-47 for the USSBS was a guy who had never before flown one. Who and why? Intriguing, no?

Let me review the thoughts crossing my mind on

into the night as I lay in bed reflecting on the exciting situation while I attempted to assess each of my higher ranking commanding officers who may have recommended or had a strong hand in having me selected for this job and their reasons for doing it.

## Lieutenant General Carl Spaatz

The top ranked Air Force General in Europe and a long shot. I consider him to be the least likely of the three candidates, solely because he's too big. Nevertheless, his name must be included, because there is still an outside possibility, he's the guy. His power in the Army Air Force military ranks was beyond question and had he personally wanted me to be given the USSBS flying job, it would have been done without any anxiety on his part about possible censure actions for having sent an unqualified pilot to the USSBS.

The only physical evidence I have that links my name with Lt Gen Carl Spaatz is the card shown earlier. On the surface, even that won't connect me with the USSBS position unless one concocts a somewhat hypothetical account or story to bridge the gap.

First a few facts. Gen Eisenhower brought Lt Gen Spaatz up from North Africa to take over the top spot of USSTAF in Jan 1944. In the previous spring (1943), he was the Deputy Air Commander of North Africa operations then later became Commander of the NW African Air Forces in Sicily. Among the units that came under his command at some point in his North African tour of duty were the two fighter Groups, the 31st and the 52nd. It's entirely logical to assume among the many conversations he must have had with his Group Commanders, he could have been informed of the problems the two Groups previously had in North Ireland in July and August 1942 Let's assume he privately disagreed, (this is entirely speculative on my part) with our high commands decision to initially equip the two Groups with old obsolete model Spitfires.

For not knowing the planes were in such poor shape maintenance wise they could possibly be excused, but they did know the British had retired the planes from combat. Speculating further, it's possible the 3-star general took a little more than casual interest in keeping track of the progress of the half dozen or so pilots that did not make the trip to North Africa at the end of 1942. I have long suspected without any concrete evidence the letter I wrote to Gen. Kane asking for Lt Wolff's recall may have been brought to Lt. Gen. Carl Spaatz's attention in a staff meeting, or for some reason was referred to his office. Honestly, I have no solid reasoning for believing that to be a fact, but if it did happen, it may have been cause enough for him to remember me.

One thing more, knowing military protocol as I do, and knowing how it's normally done, it's almost certain SHAEF received my name from USSTAF for the creation of orders to transfer my unit from Cherbourg to Le Bourget, Paris. The recommendation, of course should have originated with Gen. Kane or Col. Bateman and just been endorsed by Lt. Gen. Spaatz. On the other hand, it's possible Lt. Gen. C. Spaatz originated it himself and sent Gen. Kane a copy of his actions. I doubt if that occurred, but then, who knows? Admittedly, Lt. Gen. Carl Spaatz is a long shot.

## Brig. Gen. C.P. Kane.

A number of things, all flattering and good, happened to me after I wrote Gen. Kane asking him to recall Lt. Wolff. (1) He promptly recalled Lt. Wolff and replaced him with a much better officer. Never was I criticized or reprimanded for having written the letter or left with the impression that my actions had disappointed him in any way. (2) Approximately two months after the Lt. Wolff incident, I received a promotion in rank to Captain. (3) SHAEF HQ wrote orders around the third week of September, (immediately after my promotion) notifying me that my entire organization was being transferred from the Querqueville air base near Cherbourg to the same position at the Le Bourget air base near Paris. Essentially the orders were travel orders but since it was necessary for my unit to travel through three very active army groups, orders authored by SHAEF were a requirement. Verbally, I was also instructed to assume command of the base until the first permanent base unit arrived. SHAEF HQ would never have included my name and my unit in those orders without clearance from USSTAF. Bear in mind, there were several alternative choices of officers that could have been chosen to send on that trip to take over Le Bourget, so I've always considered it a compliment my unit was picked. Totally lacking proof, I have always believed it was Gen. Kane who submitted my name initially.

## Colonel Martin A. Bateman.

Now would be a good time and place to outline the most likely path or paper trail for the Pentagon's instructions and orders regarding the formation of the USSBS organization. First the paper or file would have been sent to Gen. Eisenhower of SHAEF. After Gen. Eisenhower and his staff had studied it, he would have added his comments and recommendations then forwarded it to Lt. Gen. Carl Spaatz, commanding General of USSTAF for action. Gen. Spaatz would have studied it, then added his comments and recommendations then forwarded it to Brig. Gen. Kane of the Air Service Command for action. At this point Gen. Kane evidently elected to take the final action on the need for a specially modified C-47 equipped with seats in the front end of the passenger cabin and a jeep in the rear. That project was assigned to one of his repair depots. He would then have added his comments and recommendations to the file and forwarded it to Col. Martin A. Bateman of the 302'nd Transport Wing for action regarding a crew.

What is not known, but which would be interesting to learn is whether Gen. Kane included in his comments to Col. Bateman his choice for a pilot, or whether Col. Bateman made the decision entirely on his own.

Could it be that the baby-faced Colonel that I stared at eyeball to eyeball from across the hall daily for several months at Southport and who I described earlier as being a serious minded military man with a dry sense of humor and a mellow side that was only occasionally detectable was really my benefactor after all? Incredible, but possible! Somebody certainly did, and he has to be a likely choice. If he did, he had guts and extreme confidence that his choice would succeed, or he risked being criticized for his choice. As commanding officer of the 302nd Transport Wing in December 1944 as well as in January 1945 he would have had access to my military record file. At least that's where it should have been maintained. The personnel records of the pilots of the 31st or the 47th Transport Groups would have been maintained and secured at their group HQ. Since the 10th airdrome Squadron was too small to be staffed in a practical manner to secure the privacy of personnel records our records would logically have been kept at Wing HQ.

When we were at Southport Col. Bateman wouldn't have had access to my file since at that time it was kept at 8th AFHQ. Perhaps when he reviewed my file in France, he concluded that my record showed I had been a skillful pilot who rightly should be flying full time. Just as importantly, he very likely read about my 52nd Fighter Group history and felt he did not disapprove or condemn me for the action I took. If he did read the file which I assume he did, he must have somewhat agreed that we were given a bad deal when we were given those old antiquated obsolete model Spitfires to fly at Londonderry, North Ireland. Truthfully, I have no idea what he really thought, as I don't recall ever having had a conversation with him about it. Could it be that the very thin mellow streak I saw in that guy was overlapped by a much thicker streak of compassion. Or put another way, just a pussycat wearing the shell of a hardnosed military man. It's hard to figure a man sometime, isn't it?

*My Flight Crew: Sgt. Bertolina on the left Captain Geisel on the right.*

The bottom line is one or more of the three individuals above put me into that USSBS pilot's seat. Which one and why, I am unable to prove because I don't know any more than what I've already told you. Frankly, it's been so many years ago I had actually forgotten all about it until just now, sitting and writing about it has brought it all back, and now I start wondering again. Who was my real benefactor?

## Maj. Poliski

The morning after I had flown a C-47 for the first time was also the morning after I'd fussed and stewed the night through trying to figure out how I got here and what to say to Gen. Sorensen. Nevertheless, I checked back in to the

USSBS HQ in London, thinking in terms my safest approach would be to keep my mouth shut. Meanwhile several more officers had checked in, including Gen. Sorensen and my two crew members. Fortunately, I was not scheduled to see the General until after I had checked in with the Operations officer, Maj. Poliski. That turned out to be a good break.

Maj. Poliski spoke with a strong accent. When he told me he spoke four languages, Polish, German, Spanish, and some English, I was able to figure out where he was from. Poland! He was an extremely friendly fellow and I liked him instantly. After talking with him for a short while I felt comfortable enough to level with him and told him my problem. I asked him if the General knew I had not been checked out on a C-47, and he replied that the General had said nothing to him about it, so he assumed he didn't know. I then asked him to please not tell the General, or the General might not want to ride with me, and I didn't want to lose that job. Maj. Poliski told me not to worry, he understood, and he knew exactly how to handle it. He claimed to have over a hundred hours on a C-47 personally and would use some excuse to take the next flight or two. No one would need to know I was riding in the co-pilot's seat to learn. To others, it would appear that I was just outranked for the left seat. Then when I felt ready, Capt. Geisel could have his rightful seat. "As a matter of fact," he said, "the General wants to go to Paris tomorrow, and so do I. I've never been there, so we'll do it in the morning, OK?"

Flying back into Le Bourget where just a few days previously I had the title of Base Operations Officer, gave me somewhat of a strange feeling, but I was looking forward to it. I wanted the fellows who formerly worked for me to see who I was hob-nobbing with now! That ought to impress them. But first, we had a landing to execute and for this one at hand, I elected to sit with my hands folded on my lap while Maj. Poliski showed me how he could land this baby. Unfortunately, it did not go well. Like so many pilots who either have faulty depth perception, or for whatever reason, lack confidence in making landings, they approach the landing area with too much speed. So, instead of simultaneously letting the wheels touch ground when stalling speed is reached, they literally fly the plane down to the runway, tail high, with full flaps, then as soon as the wheels touch, cut the throttle. The problem with this technique is that with the excess speed, there is still a lot of lift remaining in the wings, and if the wheels unexpectedly touch the runway a little too hard, a big balloon bounce occurs, and one big bounce usually begets another, then another, and another, porpoise fashion, until the plane finally slows below stalling speed. Well, this is what happened, and I said to myself, "Oh my God, now the General riding back in the passenger's compartment is going to think I landed this plane. I may have made a bad decision back there, agreeing to ride copilot. His landing technique is one I never used (well, almost never). My depth perception has always been dependably good; hence I've always landed planes, including fighters, the old-fashioned way, or the way I was first taught. On the return flight to Biggin Hall, I reached a decision.

I was going to keep my hands on the copilots steering column as we made our landing this time and do it without asking his permission. This I did, and I suspect he could feel he was getting some unsolicited help. Nevertheless, he never said a word. The end result was a perfect three-point landing, giving me courage to tell Maj. Poliski, "I'd like to take the next flight, I think I'm ready." From that point on, it was just the three men crew of myself, Capt. Geisel and Sgt. Bertolina. We flew all the USSBS flights until the end of the war, or my wedding (they occurred almost simultaneously).

Many of the USSBS professors we flew to the continent, but not all, planned to remain on the continent to work. Some followed the front, using ground transportation. In order to accomplish that, the USSBS established a few temporary forward bases as near the front as practical. They provided the essential food, shelter, and ground transportation. Most of our flights were directed to one of these points, or as near as we could get. Often, this was a difficult task to perform. There were two principle reasons for this difficulty: 1) bomb craters and 2) weather. The Allied bombing campaign had very effectively made all former military airfields unsafe to use. About the only remaining places to land safely were the small sod-covered airfields, formerly used by non-military planes. That's where we landed most often. Although I did once, by USSBS request, land in a cow pasture, complete with cows. On another flight, I gave some serious consideration to landing on an open stretch of the German Autobahn but chickened out on the final approach.

Probably the only things that handicapped our missions as much as the shortage of good landing fields, were the lack of dependable weather reports and the absence of radio navigational aids on the continent. There were no reporting Allied weather stations on the continent while the war on the continent was in its early stages, which meant the struggling weathermen in England had a severe handicap when trying to advise a pilot leaving London, what kind of weather he should expect to find on the continent. It was just an educated wild guess. As a consequence, I found their forecasts to be largely unreliable, both ways. Generally, they erred on the gloomy side, meaning I often found the weather to be better than forecast, but then there were several occasions when it was worse.

I remember flying through a hailstorm that scared the hell out of me. It was in France someplace. I had the plane on autopilot and was flying below the clouds. I could see some thin streaks of rain up ahead, but I could see sunshine through it, so I wasn't too worried. Then suddenly, I heard this WHAM. When you are flying 170 miles an hour and a piece of ice hits you, it makes a racket Then we started getting pelted by lots of hail. I had to reach a decision quickly. I knew the hailstorm was thin, so do I go on through or head back? I decided to use my fighter training and put the plane in as steep a bank as possible and turned around. Then we went around the storm and landed safely at our intended destination. When we landed, we discovered there was quite a bit of visible damage. In addition to numerous dents, the radio antennae and the sticky finger directional antennae were broken. Sgt. Bertolina was able to fix most of the problems immediately, so we were able to return safely home.

Not only were there no reporting weather stations on the continent during this wartime period, there were no dependable radio stations, either. Some radio stations would be on for a while, and then suddenly go off. None could be counted on as dependable and reliable. Dependable radio signals in the right locations were necessary to help alleviate the uncertain weather factor because the radio signals can be used to navigate. Without radio aides, navigation in the clouds becomes a guessing game. Indeed, pinpoint letdowns to a specific airfield would have been impossible had not a nearby radio station been available to home in on. Often, there wasn't any. Hence, during an unusual stretch of foul weather, I had to cancel several flights.

One morning when I arrived at Biggin Hill to take out a flight, I discovered something new had been added. Across the nose of my plane, the name MAÑANA (Spanish for "tomorrow") was blazingly painted in bright yellow. I knew it was done as a friendly needle and I only knew of one fellow who spoke with an accent like that (and had enough authority that he would dare do it), but because of my cordial relationship with Maj. Poliski, I didn't let it upset me. In fact, when I left the USSBS in early August 1945, the name MAÑANA was still on the plane's nose.

The needle notwithstanding, I would like to say I am proud of one very good record. In spite of all the strange places we landed, some in semi-treacherous terrain, and in unpredictable weather, we never had a single accident, not even a fender bender, so to speak, and no one ever got hurt, even minimally.

In actuality, most USSBS flights were of such routine nature, there is nothing much exciting or interesting that I can recall, except for the few I will share below.

Taking them in order, the first trip covers a period very early in my assignment. Actually, it was very soon after the Battle of the Bulge, but before the front reached Germany.

We landed at the Brussels municipal all-grass airfield, which, surprisingly, had not been bombed. Brussels was only about an hour's flight from London, and normally on such short flights, we would return to London immediately and come back for the passengers at a later date. But for some reason, which escapes me right now, we had to remain overnight.

A place was found for us to stay. I was told high ranking German officers had billeted there before our arrival. It was a large, very nice private home, expensively furnished, with thick, all wool carpets. I can recall admiring several paintings on the walls, but not being an art student, I had no idea of their value, or if they were genuine. But they all looked good to me. There were also several sculptured objects, even a small statue, which could have been someone's family member.

That night for some reason, I couldn't sleep well, which is unusual for me. Normally, I was a sound sleeper. Still am. But I was very uncomfortable in that house. There was something eerie about it. There was an awful lot of static electricity in that house. As you walked about, your hair would stand on end. Of course, common sense says if you combine low humidity with walking on thick wool carpets, you should expect static electricity, but somehow there seemed to be a little extra power there somewhere.

My Plane, Manana

The next morning at breakfast, I learned from Capt. Geisel he had similar thoughts about the house. Indeed, he said if we didn't return home today, he was going back to the airfield and sleep in the plane, or find somewhere else to sleep, because he wasn't going to stay in this house another night. Too many ghosts!

So what happens? Turns out we can't leave as we'd hoped. Like it or not, we had to spend another night. As evening approaches, I'm considering returning to the airfield and sleeping in the plane with Capt. Geisel (our crew always had sleeping gear stowed on the plane for emergency overnights). Then Capt. Geisel approached me and said he'd been invited to spend the night with a young lady who lived in a nearby apartment and wanted to know if it would be okay. I told him, "First find out if she has a sister. If that doesn't work out, be sure you're back here for breakfast at 6:00 tomorrow morning, because I want to be prepared to leave early."

Now I had a problem. I had to return to the plane alone if I really wanted to sleep there, or I could sleep in the haunted house again. I decided to tough it out at the house. After all, I considered myself a pretty sane and stable person. I was also someone who doesn't believe in ghosts. So, I returned to the house of gloom. The same eeriness that had been present the night before still plagued the home. But I was able to get in my beauty rest.

The next morning, Capt. Geisel arrived for breakfast right on time (with a smile on his face, I might add), and he brought along some enlightening information from his pretty hostess. She informed him the owners and former residents of the house were a Jewish family that departed suddenly without saying a single good-bye to anyone. She was very worried about them. She was hoping Capt. Geisel, being an American, could do some checking.

The whole world now knows what likely happened to the owners of that house, but I didn't know it then. Didn't even suspect. At that time, I really didn't think much about their mysterious disappearance. A lot of reasons could be given for their vanishing, particularly with a war going on. Actually, it was about another three months before our G.I.s made the grim discovery. Only then did we learn Hitler and his clan, in their sick heads, had concluded Jews belonged to an outcast and unwanted religious group (in their minds), and that exterminating them was fully justified. Shades of Genghis Kahn. Do you realize, had Hitler somehow lucked out and won the war, complete annihilation of Jews worldwide would almost certainly have taken place? It also means MY family would not exist.

I won't ever forget that house in Brussels. If ever a house was really, really haunted, that one was. But for me, that house is beyond being haunted just remembering I actually slept in their bed is haunting enough.

I mentioned previously I had to land once in a cow pasture. And it was a cow pasture, with cows. But the USSBS wanted me to deliver a crew to this spot, and there were no air bases nearby. Whatever airfields there had been close to this location were all bombed out. Usually, in a lot of places where I was scheduled to go, if there wasn't a large base nearby, there was a small civilian strip that I could use. But in this case, there was nothing nearby.

The Army had a ground crew survey the area. They found a likely field and sectioned it off. I remember flying in over the Army jeeps and trucks on the road just past the field. The cows had been herded over to one side of the field, where they were tended by some soldiers (army cowboys?). I flew over the area once, real low, inspecting the field, then came in for a landing. After landing, (which was surprisingly smooth, given the terrain), I taxied over to the waiting jeep, where my passengers disembarked Then I took off again.

Now comes a brief tale of another flight which I also recall quite vividly. This flight took pace in late March or early April of 1945, when Gen. Sorensen said he wanted to go to Burtonwood. Since Burtonwood has a lot to do with this story, a brief description of this place is needed. It was a vast depot airfield located near Liverpool (and not far from Southport), capable of upgrading, modifying, or repairing several types of planes, both bombers and fighters, at the same time. Because there was enormous pressure to accomplish this work quickly and accurately, a very large contingent of mechanics and service personnel were stationed there. Unfortunately, morale at the base was low. The cheerless, depressing neighborhood where Burtonwood was located contributed to the problem, I'm sure. The surrounding area was heavily industrialized with a forest of tall smokestacks spewing black smoke and ash from burning coal. Consequently, Burtonwood was a dark and dirty place. No one would voluntarily be stationed there, if they had a choice.

Gen. Sorensen specified he wanted to leave London around 10:00 am. We actually left Biggin Hill at 10:30, arriving at Burtonwood just in time for lunch. Being a good fellow, Gen. Sorensen invited the flight crew to have lunch with him in the VIP dining room, which was located at the rear of their immense combination cafeteria-dining hall. Entering the cafeteria, which was visibly crowded with no empty tables, we marched single file down the aisle farthest on the right (there were four aisles). Gen. Sorensen led the way, I followed, and Capt. Geisel brought up the rear. After marching about halfway up the aisle, I spotted and recognized a 2nd Lieutenant sitting alone near the aisle at one of their picnic style tables. Yes, it was Lt. Wolfe. That bastard! So, this is where they had banished him! (I loved it. Oh, how I loved it!). As I quickly marched past, I noticed his first glance was upward at the stars on the shoulder of Gen. Sorensen, then his eyes switched and he saw me, but the expression on his face didn't change one bit. It remained blank (like his brain). Neither one of us spoke, and I never missed a step.

At lunch, sitting next to Gen. Sorensen, it was on the tip of my tongue throughout the meal to say something about Lt. Wolfe, but I was troubled at the appearance of this being deliberately set-up. I've often wondered if I did the right thing, but at the time I decided to abide by the old rule: Keep quiet when in doubt. I did, and so did the General. Lt. Wolfe was not mentioned.

When lunch was over, we returned directly to our plane and took off for London. I was with Gen. Sorensen the whole time from the Biggin Hill departure till the return landing at Biggin Hill. The General conducted absolutely no business with anyone, nor talked to anyone other than the crew members. From all appearances, we flew 200 miles to Burtonwood for the sole purpose of having lunch. So, I'll leave it to the reader, was it a prearranged set-up, or a very weird coincidence? If it was a set-up, who arranged it, and why? I have always wondered and somewhat believed it might have been the very top man in the Air Service Command, Gen. Kane, certainly he had the power and the depots reported to him. Even so, it still seems highly unlikely that a man in such a high position would waste his time, thoughts and energy on something that for him, at least, was just a trivial matter. Perhaps Gen. Kane and Gen. Sorenson were buddies and Gen. Kane had relayed the story about Lt. Wolfe to him. I never found out.

\* \* \*

As the Allied front made its way into and across Germany, the USSBS organization continually advanced its Continental Headquarters as well. The largest of these headquarters, and the one where our plane made the most trips, was the one near Frankfurt, Germany. Frankfurt itself, being an all-rubble city from the fierce bombings it endured, would not have made a very desirable location for a headquarters, but just about 25 miles beyond Frankfurt, right on the Autobahn, was Bad Nauheim, which made a great location. Bad Nauheim was a small resort town, composed mostly of very picturesque hotels. Somehow, the USSBS managed to take over an entire hotel. While it's pure speculation on my part, it's not unreasonable to assume they may have inherited it the same way they obtained the Brussel's residence where I spent those two bad nights. The hotel was staffed and run by American G.I.s. It was a nice place to stay and the USSBS people were always good, congenial hosts to our flight crew. We stayed there overnight on several occasions, although we often arrived from and returned to London the same day.

The landing field itself was a sod covered pasture atop a high picturesque plateau-type hill, about 6-7 miles NW of Frankfort. It may have been Frankfort's former municipal airport. At least, it had not been bombed. Surprisingly, there were no buildings or trees around the field, just a good big open space, excellent for airplanes. Later, the Corps of Engineers installed steel mats for a runway and parking.

Even though our jeep was nearly always on board, we rarely used it when flying to Frankfurt. We used their ground transportation instead. On arrival, I'd buzz the Bad Nauheim hotel a couple of times at extremely low altitude, like ten feet above their steeple, to let them know of our imminent arrival.

The system worked so well, we knew with certainty we could depend on a staff car or two making the 25-mile trip up the Autobahn by the time we parked the plane and finished securing it. We appreciated the service since it saved us the hassle of unloading and reloading our jeep. While in those days we may have lacked the convenience of a modern-day cell phone, the buzz job was just as effective and much more fun.

It was from the Frankfurt airfield that I gave several hitchhiking liberated American POWs a free lift to London. Where they came from and how they got there, I can't say. It was different in each case. But we never turned a single one down. There was about a 2-3 week period there when I could expect to find a small handful waiting each time we landed.

As I think I mentioned earlier, one of the nice side benefits to flying for the USSBS was the fact it gave me the time and means to court my only girlfriend, Shirley Selby. It was during this period our courtship began to get serious. One of the big social events I attended during this time was the wedding of Shirley's sister, Lynda, who married the boy who lived across the street, Lionel Braham (who later became a movie producer). We also went out together several evenings, sort of double-date style.

One evening in a cab riding back from an evening out with Lynda and Lionel, I let Shirley know my marital intentions. She didn't give me a definite answer right away, but I could tell she wasn't insulted at the suggestion. It meant more time and discussion was needed to resolve some sticky issues. Number one on the list was the fact I came from a Western Kansas farm family of modest means with a Protestant Baptist background. She was a big city Jewish girl from the heart of London from an upper middle-class family (her father owned a series of retail stores). Several evenings were spent casually discussing the issue. Finally, we both concluded neither of us had such deep-seated religious convictions for it to inhibit a middle ground stance from being taken. (I guess it's true that opposites attract. Certainly, Shirley's background and mine could not have been much more opposite.)

We also agreed that if there were any children, our religious treatment of the children would be neutral. One more important point, though. Shirley was adamant. She would NEVER agree to be a farmer's wife. Even though my father, using the money I had sent home, had just purchased 240 acres the year before in my name, I agreed. That was easy! I promised if she would marry me, I'd pursue some line of work that would meet her approval.

Eventually, we agreed on all points, but before we could actually pick a wedding date, there was one more thing we had to do. We had to go through military channels and get Uncle Sam's approval.

*Wayne, Shirley and I around the time of the wedding*

Finally, with the approval in hand, we picked our date, May 10th, which was about six weeks away. Then using some of my accrued military leave, I arranged to take one week's vacation starting May 10th. The military orders granting my requests are dated April 7th, 1945. The orders also granted a railway voucher to Brighton. I assume that was our military wedding present.

Also, fortuitously somewhere in the March to early April period, an old childhood buddy, farm friend, and closest neighbor (1/2 mile), Wayne Bird, looked me up. He was a Private in the infantry, having been recently drafted and sent overseas. Following a few "good old days" visits, I offered him the job of being the best man at my wedding. He accepted.

Unknown to us at the time when we made all these marvelous plans was the war with Germany was going to end suddenly, right about the time we were to wed. VE Day (Victory in Europe) occurred on May 8th, just two days before our big day. Meanwhile, even though we had made our wedding plans, including making honeymoon reservations at a hotel in Brighton, I still had some USSBS flying to do. And that happened to include one of the most notable and unforgettable trips I ever made. I think you'll agree.

As the Russians entered Berlin, it was obvious to everyone the end was near, it was just a question of the day and hour. After Hitler committed suicide on April 30th, all fighting within the city ended the following day (May 1st), but the official and unconditional German surrender of the city to the Russians did not take place until the next day (May 2nd). USSBS Headquarters, of course, had been monitoring these events very closely because they knew some of the most important documents significant to their report would be found in Berlin. On May 2nd, I flew Gen. Sorensen to Villacoublay Airfield in Paris, where we picked up Sgt. Frost, early in the morning. From there, we flew to Bad Nauheim (Frankfurt) where we spent the night.

Just a short footnote here that is an interesting sidelight. On January 2001, while rummaging through an old wallet that dated back to World War II which I had found in my equally old military 201 file, I discovered an interesting document. I found the original approved flight plan for a flight from Station A-42 (Villacoublay, near Paris) to Frankfort. It was dated May 2nd, 1944. In addition to showing the weatherman's forecast for the route, it also listed the people making the flight with me. They were: General Sorenson, Captain Wait, Captain Geisel, Master Sergeant Bertolina, and Master Sergeant Frost. Why Sgt. Frost was on board, I do not recall, if I even ever knew. I do not remember him. My best guess, and it's only a guess, was that he was a German interpreter.

After arriving at our Bad Nauheim USSBS hotel-HQ, Gen. Sorensen inquired and learned it would be safe to resume our flight to Berlin. Thereupon, he announced we would continue our flight early in the morning.

The flight to Berlin from Frankfurt took about $1\frac{1}{2}$ hours. Like so many European municipal airfields at the time, Tempelhof (the airfield in Berlin) had no runways. It was all grass. I had never encountered an airfield before that was shaped quite like Tempelhof. Being almost circular was the nice part about its physical set-up. The bad part was the 2-3-4 story buildings that completely ringed it. No matter the wind direction, a pilot could always land and take off directly into the wind, but he also had high buildings to worry about on both landing and take-off. Tempelhof was large enough, though, that C-47s had ample room to spare. Incidentally, I never saw a single bomb crater there. As a matter of fact, I saw very few in the parts of Berlin I visited. On the other hand, I did see a lot of buildings that had been pulverized by Russian artillery, like Hitler's Reichskawzlei, for instance. Perhaps I was subconsciously expecting Tempelhof to resemble the condition in which I found Le Bourget when I first arrived there about eight months previous. But actually, the damage wasn't comparable at all. La Bourget was much, much more severe. But then some allowance should be made for the fact the Germans would give top priority to repairing damage in Berlin.

As we approached the field, I saw another C-47 on the ground, so I know we weren't the first to arrive, but we might have been the second. I really don't know for certain, because someone could have landed, dropped off passengers, and then taken off again. But I am confident we were among the earliest Americans to arrive. Just observing the Russian behavior and demeanor upon our arrival gave one that impression. Immediately as I stepped off the plane, I had an astonishing encounter with the first person that stepped forward to greet us. It was a Russian officer dressed in a long overcoat that almost touched the ground, who said in fairly good English, "Hello, welcome to Berlin." But what followed was an even bigger surprise.

He offered me a thousand dollars for the chronograph wristwatch I was wearing. Like the fool I am, I turned him down. Had he offered me $50, maybe even $30, I would have yanked it off and handed it to him. But a thousand dollars for a watch, I could replace in the PX for $19.95?!! Something was horribly wrong! Perhaps the Rubles were counterfeit, but then I remembered having a wild money exchanging experience with a French banker concerning the French Franc, so maybe his offer was on the up and up. The Russian didn't get too discouraged with my turndown; he followed up his first offer with a bid of $100 for a pack of Lucky Strike cigarettes in my pocket. That I handed to him, gratis. I had a whole carton containing 10 packs in the cabin of my plane that I paid about $2 for. What's going on here, I wondered? Are the Russians starving for American goods and endowed with lots of money to spend?

Nearly an hour later, another American who had been in the plane that preceded me to Berlin, informed me why the Russian soldiers were throwing so much money around. According to his story, the Russian soldiers had not been paid for a very long time, something like three years or more. Then all of a sudden, the Russian Government came into a lot of money and paid their troops all their back pay. Driving by in my jeep, we could see Russian soldiers carrying their money (or something) around in sacks. Not little sacks, I mean BIG sacks – as in Santa Clause size sacks! They were similar to, but larger than our G.I. duffel bags. Believe it or not, I saw at least two dragging their sacks behind as they walked. At first, I thought the sacks contained dirty clothes, but the other American insisted, "No. Those aren't clothes, that's a sack of Russian Rubles." I don't know how he could be so certain unless he actually peeked inside a sack. Perhaps a Russian soldier told him. This American told me he could speak a little Russian.

As we drove by the Tiergarten, a very large park,

we witnessed several clusters of Russian soldiers in their long great coats huddled in circles exactly like a series of American style football huddles. Curious as to what they were all looking at, we stopped and went over to the closest cluster. To our surprise we found in the center of the huddle was a squatting Russian with a magnifying glass examining a watch with its back off, counting the jewels. Obviously, these Russian soldiers had a very deep passion for watches! Now, the $1000 watch offer began to make some sense.

Across the street from the park, Tiergarten, was Hitler's Bunker[28], which is what we had really come to see. Surprisingly, smoke was still coming out of it! I hadn't ex-

---

[28] **Hitler's Bunker (from *Wikipedia*):** As the war began to wind down, and German's fate became clearer, Hitler retreated to a bunker – which was essentially a large underground bomb shelter- that had been constructed next to his Government building. The bunker had originally been built in 1948, but Hitler had recently increased its size and built deeper to withstand stronger bomb blasts. The bunker was located under the garden of Reischskanzlie.

Hitler, even as he became more and more mentally unstable, ran Germany's war effort from this bunker during the final days of the war. He would spend his final days issuing order to his defeated armies, while dining on meals prepared by his vegetarian cook.

On April 29th, Hitler married Eva Braun, his long-time mistress. Later that same day, Hitler had his favorite dog… killed. The next day, with Russian troops a block away, Hitler and his newlywed wife committed suicide deep within the bunker.

Eva killer herself by ingesting poison. Hitler died of a gunshot through the mouth.

The bodies were taken to the surface and placed in a bomb crater, where aides burned their bodies, along with the bodies of 14 others. Dirt was then poured into the crater, forming a shallow grave…

pected that, but the smoke wasn't thick enough to prevent me from going down to have a good look. I was hoping to find a souvenir, but I was disappointed. It was barren. Apparently, there had been enough Russians ahead of me with the same idea to clean it out. The bunker, itself, was unremarkable, except for its historical significance. I can remember there being bare walls and very little furniture. The furniture that was there was very austere, nothing ornate. It was pretty much like any other bomb shelter – except for the fact that this one had been used by Adolph Hitler!

So, I turned my scavenging attention to the severely Russian shelled building next door, the Reichskanzlei (Hitler's Headquarters), and after poking around through the rubble, managed to find a box containing eight-dozen German medals. I think I have five left. My kids took most to school for "show and tell."

As we were boarding our plane for our return flight to London, Gen. Sorensen commented we would have to return the next day. While he didn't elaborate, I assumed some of the documents he wanted weren't available today but would be tomorrow. That was okay with me, and it gave me an idea. 'If we're returning tomorrow,' I reasoned, 'why not take advantage of the Russian's mania for watches and capitalize on it?' As soon as we landed at London, I immediately hit a couple of pawnshops and cleaned them out of their best-looking watches. How many watches I had in total, I don't remember, but I put them all in a white shoe box, and the shoe box was about ¼ full.

The next day, when we landed at Berlin, Gen. Sorensen changed his itinerary slightly. On the previous day's flight, as on several other trips, our flight crew was allowed to use the jeep while he rode with someone else in their vehicle. (Generals usually receive guest-like treatment). On this second trip, however, he surprisingly announced that we would all ride together in our jeep.

That came as a blow and effectively killed my plans to sell an assortment of watches to the Russians. Never would I even consider trying to sell those watches in the General's presence! If nothing else, it would be disrespectful and might embarrass him. The shoe box then remained under the pilot's seat with my other personnel effects.

That was good enough for me. I'm just an ordinary aerial taxi driver pilot from Western Kansas, who was dumb enough to bring a shoe box partially filled with watches to Berlin to sell to the Russians, then wise enough to haul the whole lot back to London to sell back to the pawn shops at a big loss. It was a great merchandising lesson, and the end to my career in the black-market.

Not only was that my last flight to Berlin, it essentially marked the beginning of the end of all of my USSBS flying, and as to General Sorensen, it was definitely our last flight together. When I returned from my honeymoon vacation (around May 17th), the General had already departed for the U.S. The war was over, and everyone wanted to get home as quickly as possible, including me. While I was on my honeymoon, Maj. Poliski flew "MAÑANA" in my place.

VE Day was May 8th and a holiday for everyone. My childhood friend, Wayne Bird, came by and we celebrated for some time together. He even spent the night sleeping on the floor of my apartment. He was comfortable, though, as he had the benefit of a military air mattress and a sleeping bag. The one and only bed in my apartment was undersized and neither of us fancied sleeping with the other, particularly in such close quarters.

For musical entertainment, we listened to the single phonograph record I had, which had been left behind by the apartment's previous occupant. It consisted of four harmonica players playing the tune "Smoke Gets in Your Eyes." I listened to that record so many times that even today when I hear that song, I am reminded of that Richmond apartment.

OK, now we're up to May 10th. The BIG, BIG day. Our wedding day! Will anything go wrong? Read on.

Shirley and I agreed we would have a very small wedding in a Justice of the Peace's office. The only guests invited were Shirley's immediate family members – her parents, three sisters, and a brother. On my side were my best man, Wayne Bird, and my flight crew only! That's all, nobody else.

So, who is present at zero hour when the wedding is scheduled to start? Well, there was Wayne Bird, my flight crew, and myself. There was also a surprise uninvited guest, Major Poliski. But that was it! Shirley and all the members of her family were no shows.

Ten minutes later and there's still no sign of Shirley or any member of her family. Now I'm impatiently pacing the floor and giving serious consideration to taking a long one-way walk. So, who puts his arm around my shoulder and tells me to calm down and that everything's going to be all right? None other than my uninvited guest, Maj. Poliski. He's explaining to me my bride-to-be and her family must be having unexpected problems. "If she wasn't coming, she or someone from her family would have called," he reasoned. "Just be patient. They're coming!" he counseled.

I listened to him and calmed down enough to wait awhile longer. My patience paid off. Major Poliski saved my marriage before it even started.

It was another ten minutes before Shirley and her family, minus her father, arrived.

The explanation given me when they finally arrived was they had a serious unexpected last-minute problem with her dress. The fact her father didn't come was not a surprise and had not been a factor. I already knew he objected to the wedding. However, considering he subsequently gave me as a wedding present, an expensive 14K gold watch (which I still have), and three thousand dollars cash (which I don't have), and later, after I'd departed for the States, he bribed a commercial ship's captain to deliver his daughter to New York; I'd say his objections weren't too objectionable.

But going back to the wedding itself, I'd have to say the jury is still out seeking an answer to the question, "would there even have been a wedding had not an uninvited guest not showed up?" Personally, I really don't know, but I doubt it. I know I was upset and was ready to walk out. Neither Wayne Bird nor anyone in my crew would have tried to stop me. I know that. Only Maj. Poliski tried.

When I returned from my honeymoon, there wasn't much USSBS flying to do, particularly now the big mover and shaker, Gen. Sorensen, was gone, but there was a little. Most of my flying seemed to be as a cargo hauler for various officer's clubs, e.g. to France for Champaign, and to Northern Scotland for Scotch Whiskey. There was one flight though, that involved my new wife that was noteworthy.

Flying assignments with our C-47 became so dead and inactive, a crew member suggested we take the dates or girlfriends of the crew members for a ride. This sounded good to me, so we did. It was a beautiful day for it, so we just cruised around Southern England sightseeing. We even buzzed the beaches between Bournemouth and Brighton. Then I allowed Shirley to come up and sit in the co-pilot's seat while Capt. Geisel went back and joined his date. I explained to her about what the instruments indicated and how they related to the plane. I even let her fly and steer the plane. Unfortunately, she misunderstood my lesson, and while I wasn't paying attention, put the plane into a modest climb that looked steeper than it was, but it got her a little worked up.

After we'd cruised around for a little over an hour, I asked Shirley to go back and get Capt. Geisel so he could help me land the plane, which she did, and he did. As I was leaving the cockpit after landing, I noticed someone had made a mess in the passenger section. A look at the faces told me who did it. My wife's face was the palest.

In all the flights I made, and all the passengers who rode with me in WW2 in all kinds of weather, she was the only one (as far as I know) who actually got airsick.

In mid-July, a Col. Wiggons of San Angelo, Texas, approached me saying the USSBS organization in both England and Continental Europe, was being phased out, and he inherited the job of closing it down and locking the door, but he thought he could successfully drag the operation out over a reasonable length of time and asked if I would consider passing on my priority to return home and stay behind to fly the plane. He said, "Using that plane with our clearance and you flying it, we can make a fortune in the black market, then you can go home later." My answer was very quick and from the heart.

"Thanks, but no thanks. Please understand, while your offer is appreciated, making a lot of money is really not a top priority of mine, particularly at this time. Right now, I just want to go home and see my parents. I haven't seen them in over three years, and I want them to meet my new wife. I'm proud of her."

Perhaps, had I known it was going to take so long getting home, I'd have accepted his offer, made a fortune, and still made it home at the same time . . . Just kidding.

# POST WAR

In early August, I was relieved from the USS3S and transferred to a North Scotland holding area, where a pool of Air Force personnel were being held awaiting a flight home via returning planes, mostly B-17s and B-24s. It was near the end of August before I was able to catch a ride on a B-17 to Iceland (it was my first and only ride in the Flying Fortress). Before departing Scotland, I phoned Shirley to inform her I finally had a ride and told her to be sure not to miss that "War Brides Boat." (After the US troops had been returned home via troop ships, a "War Brides Boat" was scheduled to take the war brides to their new country, probably about when winter set in.)

Meanwhile, because of bad weather at our next scheduled stop on our flight home, Goose Bay, Canada, we were marooned on the island of Iceland for a full three weeks. I about went stir crazy sitting around drinking cokes and listening to the record "Sentimental Journey" with some fellow Air Force fliers. Unfortunately, we had no telephone link (at that time) from the air base where we were located to either England or the USA, so there was no way to let relatives know where we were and why.

Near the end of September, the weather at Goose Bay cleared enough so we could take off. The weather was good all the way across the Atlantic and we had an excellent view of the Southern tip of Greenland. It looked just like the map shows it. When we landed at Goose Bay though, it was snowing, and it continued to snow for several days, stranding me again. Finally, on October 3rd, we left Goose Bay and landed at Bangor, Maine, where I immediately called home to Protection, Kansas.

After talking a while, exchanging some pleasantries with my mother on the phone, my mother innocently asked, "Would you like to say hello to your wife?" I didn't know how to answer that. I was speechless. What did she mean?

When Shirley said "Hello," I was still speechless. How could she possibly be in Protection? I was flying home and the last I knew when I left England, she didn't even have any prospect for a ride, other than the "War Bride Boat", which wasn't scheduled till much later in the fall.

Apparently, Shirley's father had gone to the shipyard and talked to merchant ship's captain about her riding to New York with them. Back in those days, merchant ships (freighters) were allowed to bring up to five passengers with them. After a long search, her dad finally ran across a willing Captain and bribed him to take Shirley. I'm not sure if he did this because he loved his daughter so much – or was just that eager to get her out of the country. (Just kidding, I know it was the former).

There was another war bride on the boat whom Shirley befriended, although they lost contact with each other upon reaching the States. I'm sure they were both more than a little frightened and yet excited at the same time about the adventure on which they were embarking. They were the only passengers on the ship. Being a freighter, the ship was not exactly built to accommodate the needs of passengers, and certainly wasn't built for comfort. But the crew was friendly, and they made the best of it. Unfortunately, they went through a bad storm that was very rough. As a result, she got really seasick on the trip.

When they got to New York, Shirley only had $20 because that is all England would allow people to take out of the country. Nor was there anyone in New York to meet her or for her to stay with, as no one knew she was coming. And she didn't know anyone in the States. But she now had family here – my family. So, Shirley wired my folks, telling them her situation, and asking for some money, which they immediately sent.

Now armed with some cash, (and a little went a very long way back then), Shirley bought the train tickets that would bring her to Protection and my family. But there was plenty of time before the train, so she decided to do some shopping.

The war had taken its toll on London and the British economy, making shopping very limited. But now Shirley found herself in another of the world's great shopping markets, with a little cash and a little time, and a whole lot more choices of things to buy than what she had been used to during the war. She was like a kid in a candy shop! So, she went shopping.

Shirley claims today (fifty-six years later) she only bought stockings and stuff for her in-laws. I believe she did buy lots of presents for her new in-laws. But I seem to recall her splurging on a few wardrobe items for herself, as well.

To get to Protection, Shirley took a train from New York to Wichita, Kansas. From there, she had to ride a spur line to Protection. There were only about two cars on the spur line. We called the train the "Doodle Bug."

She arrived in Wichita in the afternoon, but the train for Protection wasn't to leave until about midnight or one in the morning. Of course, when Shirley first got into the station in Wichita after a very long train trip, she made her way to the ladies' restroom. There she met someone she recognized simply from my description of her. It was my sister's sister-in-law, Velmarie Riner, whose brother, G.T., had married my sister, Doris. G.T. was in the Navy at this time.

Of course, to make things more interesting, Velmarie had another sister, Ida Mae Riner, whom I used to date. Ida Mae and I were close in age.

Shirley and Velmarie recognized each other without ever seeing one another before. Shirley went up to her and said, "You're Velmarie Riner, aren't you?" Velmarie replied, "And you're Junior's wife!"

Velmarie was returning to Protection, so they would be taking the train together. They had a great trip together to Protection. Of course, Velmarie proceeded to fill Shirley on all my past history with women. Everything I didn't want her to know.

When she got off the train, my parents and youngest sister, Doris, were there to meet her. Doris and she became great friends. Doris was so sweet to her when she arrived and made her feel welcome and part of the family. (The rest of the family was likely very occupied as this was a very critical time for farmers to get the wheat planted).

I've always admired my wife's courage during this period. Here she left her home, her family, her country, and her faith and set off for a world totally foreign to her in just about every way. She knew no one – except by the descriptions of them furnished by me. And the one person she did know, me, wasn't there to be with her. And no one knew where I was or when I would be returning. And, of course, you could not get much more of an opposite to London than Protection, Kansas. At least they spoke the same language – sort of. Further, back then, overseas calling was very problematic and expensive. And, of course, there was no internet!

The exact date Shirley arrived at my parents' home is only a guess, but it probably was somewhere around four to five days before I called home on October 3rd. Unfortunately, my frustratingly slow trip home was not over. It took another stressful three to four days to get home. Had it not been for the fact as a returning serviceman I was required to go through Ft. Dix, which is located in New Jersey, it's very likely I could have gone to the nearest air base equipped with C-46's or C-47 s and hitched a ride to Wichita or somewhere near home in a matter of hours. As it was, my journey homeward was destined to be fraught with further problems and delays.

Coming home via train seemed agonizingly slow, having to clear Ft. Dix first, spend a night there, then spending a second night on a Pullman car between St. Louis and K.C. But the worst break occurred because of a most unlikely fact. I was the highest-ranking military officer on board our train leaving Ft Dix. Now you would have thought that would have entitled me to some special privileges, but it did not. Instead, at the checkout desk I was presented with a packet containing the military personnel file of each enlisted man traveling on the train and was told that I had the responsibility of delivering each soldier and his file to the military police at either the St Louis or Ft. Leavenworth post, whichever was applicable.

At St. Louis I dropped off about twenty soldiers and still had a dozen left to take to K.C. when we left St Louis around midnight. Unfortunately, when we arrived at the Union Station in Kansas City early the next morning, I was a man short. We left St. Louis with twelve soldiers and twelve files, but we arrived in KC with twelve files and only eleven soldiers.

It was mystifying, inasmuch as the train made no stops between St. Louis and K.C. and I had made a careful check when leaving St. Louis. So, what could have happened to him? No one on our particular Pullman car could shed any light on his surprising absence. To expedite matters because we had to move on, I left the missing soldier's file with the Military Police unit at the KC Union Station along with my report and took the remaining soldiers on a local commuter train to Ft Leavenworth.

As I was still troubled by the missing soldier's whereabouts, I made it a point to return to the Military Police unit located on the mezzanine of the K.C. Union Station on my way back from Ft. Leavenworth to see if they had located the missing soldier. They had. A railroad inspection section crew found his mangled body early that morning on the tracks about eighty miles east of KC. We knew he had been doing some drinking in St Louis before we left there (as we all had, including me and my one scotch), but no one knew him well enough to account for his behavior and actions. Our assumption was that for some unknown reason during the night he left his Pullman bunk bed and attempted to enter the railway car trailing our car and somehow fell between the cars. Lacking a witness, there is no way of ever knowing exactly what happened.

Upset and feeling some guilt over the fact I'd lost a soldier on my watch, a soldier who was also returning home from overseas, I asked the MP's to give me his parents address from his file so I could pen them a brief consolatory note. It was all I could think of to do. Then on a little more sobering note, I boarded a train for my 375-mile final leg home. I can only imagine his family's anguish - going from the jubilation in knowing he was returning home safely from the war, only to have him die in the most tragic of circumstances.

The military granted me a 30-day vacation, three weeks of which were spent getting reacquainted at home. After all, I'd been gone for three and half years, and I couldn't help thinking of the Rip Van Winkle story. It was truly amazing at how much some people had changed and aged in that relatively small span of time, particularly my dad. He looked many years older. It gave me such a shock when I first saw him. I thoughtlessly said something about him showing his age, then immediately was sorry when I saw the hurt in his eyes. The war years must have been tough on him. He had prospered though, having bought a lot of new farm acreage and was now working his tail off trying to do a good job farming. Because of the war, very little outside farm labor had been available. About the only person he was able to depend on for help was my kid brother Merle, and he was about to lose him. While I was gone Merle had surprisingly grown to college age and was preparing to enroll at The University of Kansas (KU)[29]. Wow! Furthermore, in my age group, nearly all my school classmates were gone now, having scattered to all parts of the globe.

Many physical and material changes were noticeable as well. Some were a surprise. My parents had bought the farm a mile north of where we had formerly lived and had moved into a better farmhouse. With electricity too! I knew about the farm purchase. The electricity was a surprise. I learned practically all farmhouses now had electricity. When I left in 1942, none did. FDR's Rural Electrification Act had gone full speed during the war. As a result, practically every farmhouse was now equipped with refrigerators and all the usual household appliances, even air conditioning in a few cases.

Yes, numerous changes had been made while I was gone, but there was one change everyone had become accustomed to seeing every year before the war, but had not been made during the war years, and that was new car models. Right after Pearl Harbor all auto assembly lines were shut down and the factories converted to producing war goods. When this happened some people, particularly a few farmers, hoarded their last new car purchase, parking it in a garage or a barn and drove their pickup or truck instead. Gasoline was rationed anyway. That presented me with an opportunity while I was home. I was able to buy a

---

[29] Editor's Note:  He picked the best school to go to.  I am a proud two-time alumnus.  Go Jayhawks.

very low mileage four door Nash sedan that had rot been driven for several months. Lucky me! But it was evident the farmer felt he was making a benevolent and a patriotic gesture by selling it to a returning serviceman who obviously needed it. And I really did appreciate it. Shirley and I needed a car to drive to California to my next assignment.

I had orders to report to an air base near Santa Ana, California in early November 1945. Consequently, the final week of my vacation was spent leisurely traveling to California as sort of an impromptu sightseeing trip for both Shirley and me. Our trip coursed through Albuquerque, Phoenix, Las Vegas, then finally Southern Calif. My, how that area around the Cal-Aero flying school at Ontario, Cal. had developed and grown! And all that growth took place in just four years. I was amazed!

We weren't stationed in Southern California very long, maybe less than a month, but long enough to take in a football game between USC, (or was it UCLA?), and Oregon State. That was a big experience for Shirley. Not the game, necessarily, because she didn't understand it, this being the first American football game she had ever attended. While I was trying to watch the game, she spent most of her time scanning the crowd and made more than one comment regarding seeing so many women wearing full length fur coats while they were setting next to a man dressed in short sleeve shirts. Having been there before attending flying school I was familiar with the scene, so I tried to explain that it was a combination of factors. For instance, some of the people here are a little bit flaky anyway and the Southern California weather is so ideal any choice of dress is both acceptable and comfortable. Actually though, the student rooting section probably impressed her the most, with the flash cards being held up spelling witty messages. She had never witnessed a production like that in England. (USC had a good team that year, they ended ranked 11th in the country).

One day Shirley and I went into the Santa Ana business district looking for an Army Navy store. I needed some accessories for my uniform. We finally found a store, it was a small place, perhaps 15 by 20 ft, but it had the items I needed. While there, the proprietor detected Shirley's strong English accent and asked what part of England she was from. After she told him London, he pressed for what part of the town. When she informed him, it was Staverton Road of the West End, he excitedly exclaimed he had a relative who lived on Staverton Road and he corresponded with the family quite regularly. Finally, it was determined his relative lived almost directly across the street from where Shirley lived, and Shirley was certain her parents knew the family quite well. What a small world! Immediately after leaving the store she hurriedly dashed off a letter to her Mother telling her about the incident, but due to a misunderstanding about the correct postage, her letter did not go out airmail, it went regular mail, which meant it took about two weeks or more to reach her parents. (In those days letters had to be marked 'Air Mail' and a special rate paid, or they went by train and ship). Meanwhile, Shirley received a letter from her Mother explaining she had been hearing stories from her neighbor for years about their rich relative that lived in Southern California and couldn't get over the unbelievably exciting odd happenstance we actually got to meet him. She said her neighbor just now called and told her about it. "And, wasn't it nice of him to entertain you and Johnny on his yacht like he did?"

From Southern California we motored halfway across the country to our next assigned base at Ellington Field near Houston, Texas. Our orders, dated 1 Dec. 1945, said we were to report on 9 Dec.

During our brief stay in Houston, Shirley and I shared the rental of a house in Pasadena, a suburb east of Houston, with another pilot, Dale Sauers, and his wife. About the only thing the whole gang of us did there was to entertain ourselves! We did very little flying. It was almost a daily occurrence for one couple of our newfound gang to go to Texas City on the coast and buy a bushel of shrimp right off a fishing boat for the sum of one dollar, then we'd go to the loser's house to boil them (they smelled), then go to another couple's house for the feast and to party.

It was here at Houston I began to suspect something would soon have to change. It had to. There were more pilots and other officers milling about the base than there were enlisted men. The pilots were hanging on because they loved flying and the pay was much better than they could hope to find on the outside. As a matter of fact, the civilian market had already absorbed about all the military men it could handle comfortably so things were beginning to slow.

Shirley and I discussed the matter. We agreed we wanted to raise a family and we agreed moving from base to base was not the preferred way to raise children. Furthermore, I was getting tired of the constant party mode. Then right in the middle of our ongoing discussion I received orders dated 12 Feb '46 to move again, this time it was to Langley Field, near Newport News, Virginia.

In Virginia we rented a room in a house in Newport News. About the only happening of any significance during our stay there concerned the sudden disappearance of a pair of earrings I had bought Shirley for Christmas the previous year while I was stationed near Paris. The landlady was our prime suspect inasmuch as Shirley knew exactly where she put them. We politely asked the landlady if she had seen them. She hadn't. Years later I tried to replace them by having a jeweler make a pair exactly as I'd remembered them. Unfortunately, that turned out to be one of my disasters. The finished product did not resemble the original in the slightest.

In mid-April we learned we were moving again. This time we were sent to Selfridge Field, Michigan where we lasted three days, hardly long enough to completely unpack, or to get our clothes back from the cleaners. Selfridge Field in turn, furnished us with orders transferring us to an air base at Champaign, Urbana, Ill. where a record was set for the shortest assignment. We lasted one night. We definitely didn't have time to completely unpack before we hit the road again. We were putting a lot of miles on that old Nash, going coast to coast, but it held up good. This last time we traveled to a new air base near Knob Noster, Mo. which is about sixty-five miles east of Kansas City. We lasted longer there, about nine months. It was also my final active duty assignment.

While the airbase was new and located near Knob Noster, the military for some reason, perhaps it was because they didn't like the name Knob Noster, chose to call it the Sedalia Air Force Base at Warrensburg, Mo. All three municipalities were on US highway 50. Warrensburg was about ten miles to the west. Knob Noster was right by the main gate. Sedalia was a much larger town about eighteen miles eastward and was the town where many of the officers chose to live.

When we first arrived at the air base Shirley and I rented a small cramped apartment in Warrensburg but after about three weeks we moved to Sedalia where we lucked out and found a very nice apartment located over a two-car garage at 605 S. Missouri St. We were to be stationed at the Warrensburg air base from the end of April 1946 through Jan 22,1947, but because Shirley was pregnant, we continued living in our Sedalia apartment until the end of April 1947.

At Warrensburg AFB we flew C-46's, a twin-engine plane with larger engines than the C-47. It was also faster, had a slightly larger fuselage, and could carry a heavier payload. Fortunately, at that time Warrensburg AFB had more than enough planes for all pilots to get in an adequate number of hours of flying time. That was good for morale. Not only does the Warrensburg AFB still exist today, it's become a very important base. The last word I heard, which was on network news about fifty-five years after I left there, long range flying wing bombers were flying out of there.

While living at Sedalia, we had a very active social life, albeit mostly military connected. Shades of Houston! The group we hob-nobbed with were much like the rat pack. There were the Ringheims, the Kowalkowskis, and the Menefies, plus several others whose names I've forgotten. Ringheim was probably the most outstanding character of the group. He was gifted with good humor and full of fun-loving antics. Nevertheless, his wife wasn't overly impressed, she would lock him out of their apartment about once a month, and he would then come over to our apartment and sleep on our couch. They always managed to kiss and make up. The problem, I think, was nothing more than the fact both he and his wife, like the rest of us, were feeling some pressure due to the uncertainty of what the future might have in store.

This fun-loving group of officers were all golfers too, and that's where I was first introduced to the game. We played on a local 'cow pasture' golf course, complete with cows. The cows took care of 100% of the grass trimming. No mechanical mowing machine had ever been in that pasture, so fairways and rough were identical except for the topography. It was a nine-hole layout featuring sand greens but by having two sets of tee boxes on each hole, so one could play it as an 18-hole course. This hard nose group played the game beyond USGA rules. They played the ball down everywhere. The ball couldn't be touched until the sand green was reached. The only exception to that strict rule came in that rare case when a ball stopped in a pile of fresh cow manure. We played that as a water hazard. You had the option of hitting it out, (which I don't recall anyone ever doing), or taking a two-club length drop at a cost of one stroke. (In some cases. the original ball was left behind). Since I learned to play the game playing it down in very inhospitable conditions and enjoyed it so much, I still think that's the way the game should be played at all times. I don't believe in winter rules and I think our Pros are providing the wrong kind of leadership in being allowed to lift clean and place whenever their course gets wet and sloppy. Rough, tall grass, wet conditions, what's wrong with that, it was all part of our fairway. So were cockleburs, sandburs and other sticker weed patches, but we had fun, and we learned to take the bad with the good. It was all part of the game.

Green fees were twenty-five cents, but only if there was someone at the gate to collect, and usually there wasn't. At better 18-hole public courses with mowed fairways and grass greens, the fees were fifty cents, and someone was always there to collect. (Oddly enough a new golf ball cost roughly the same amount in those days as the green fee. That is something that's changed over the years. Can you imagine how sparse the attendance would be today at each golf course if each new golf ball cost the same price as the green fee)? After I'd been there about three months, I liked the game so much I joined the Sedalia Country Club. They had excellent fairways and bent grass greens. Monthly dues were $6. (Nowadays the taxes on dues easily exceed that).

In September we learned Shirley was pregnant. Her Doctor said the baby should arrive approximately April 4, 1947. Suddenly everything changed. Now we had to stop all this partying and playing around and get serious about making some important decisions. Like how do we want to raise our family we've just started? What will it be, Air Force, or civilian life? Essentially, she and I agreed the military's constant movement of personnel from base to base was a major negative. It inhibits one from taking roots and we felt the best environment for raising and educating our children the way we wanted it done would be to become firmly established in some community with the comforting knowledge we would very likely remain there.

Even though I verbally agreed to it, I'll have to

admit in looking back on it, I was probably a little slow about taking action. After all, I was doing what I loved doing the most, flying. (Plus, golf). And the pay was great. I couldn't possibly come close to equaling an Air Force Captain's pay, starting at the bottom at a new job in civilian life. I knew that, because I did a little checking, casually of course, because I failed to see any real urgency. That is, I didn't until I received the following new military orders, from our HQ at Lowery Field, Colorado, dated 8 November 1946:

"After careful consideration, it has been decided to recommend that you be relieved from active duty under the provisions of Section II of Circular 44, WD, 1946. This recommendation is based on a reduction in organizational strength of officers of this command due to stringent limitations that have been placed on budgetary allowances allotted to the AAF. Therefore, it is suggested you make necessary arrangements that will be required for your return to inactive status. This action has not been taken on the basis of military performance you have rendered but because of required reduction in the current officer strength of this command.

"It is regretted that this action is mandatory, and I wish to express the appreciation of the commanding General of the Army Air Forces for the honorable and faithful service you have rendered during your tour of active duty. Provided you become a member of the Officers Reserve Corps you may apply to the Adjutant General for recall to active duty at a later date, should a need arise. Widest publicity will be given through appropriate press releases when vacancies occur."

All my buddies received a copy of the same order. Subsequent orders placed an arbitrary release date of Jan. 22, 1947. Oddly enough, about thirty days after being told I had to leave the service, I received my promotion to the rank of Major. Apparently, that was the Air Force's good will, going away gift, or maybe it was a present for agreeing to join the Air Force Reserves.

OK, now that we know that the Air Force is definitely out, and farming is out (I'd agreed to that before the wedding, remember?) So, what to do?

Being an experienced pilot and desiring to remain in the profession the logical place to look for a job would be with the airlines, right? Well I tried, in fact I made applications with every airline that flew in and out of KC at that time, and a few that didn't. Some of them don't even exist today. But every one of them had the same minimum requirement that eliminated me immediately. I was too short. Every airline required their pilots to be at least 5' 9" tall. I am 5' 7 1/2". At the end of the war several thousand experienced pilots were released from the service. So many, the airlines could absorb only a fraction of the pool available, hence the airlines could set almost any standard they wished, including blue eyes and blond hair if they so desired, and still have more qualified applicants than they could use.

Remember my mentioning Hugh Chance earlier? He was my ex-college roomie, whom I talked into joining me in taking flying lessons while we were both students at Ft. Hays St College way back in 1940. Well, in desperation I even called him (he lived in the Denver area) to see if he could use his influence in getting a waver for me to fly with United. He said he would try, and for me to come on out. He'd personally take me to see their personnel manager. Hugh said the manager was a pretty nice guy and if approached right, might respond in a positive manner. So out to Denver I went. Even though Hugh had been working for United for less than six years, he had already become one of their top pilots and as you might guess, one of their highest paid. He was also a good persuasive debater, so with Hugh volunteering to lend his support I considered my chances to be worth investing in a 600-mile trip.

After a rather short get acquainted meeting in the

personnel managers office in which he attentively listened to Hugh's praiseworthy speech on my behalf he suddenly stood up and said to me "Let's go down the hall to our examining room. If you are within a half an inch or less of minimum maybe, we can do something. Hugh has convinced me that you can fly as good as any six-footer we've got. Now let's see if you can measure up where it counts."

He had me stand on the scales in my stocking feet which negated the thick soled shoes I wore for the occasion and as he carefully measured my height I took a deep breath and stretched myself to my maximum height but I could tell from the lack of a smile on his face it had not been enough. "I'm sorry" he said, "you're not even close. If I made an exception in your case, you and me both would be walking the streets next week looking for a job. United is dead serious about this minimum height thing. Sorry."

Hugh invited me to spend the night at his house, which I gladly accepted. It was good to meet his family (he had two sons) and talk over old times, which we did until late that night. Being an old ex-western Kansas farm boy Hugh evidently still preferred living the rural life. He had bought a quarter section of land (160 acres), near Longmont and had his pasture stocked with Appaloosa horses, a relatively new breed at that time. Those horses were his hobby, he loved them. That evening while we were having our 'good old days' conversation he went to a desk drawer and pulled out two separate monthly checks from United which he hadn't even bothered to deposit yet. Each check exceeded eight thousand dollars, which meant his annual take in 1946 was about $100,000, which he did not deny.[30]

---

[30] Remember, though, the high taxes. At 90%, his take-home was only $10,000/year. Big difference!

Not bad! Back in 1946 that amount of money would buy a whole lot of anything. In the intervening six years since I last saw him, he had done very well. Hugh explained he was successful in achieving the high pay level he was getting by having made bids to fly the most hazardous routes between Denver and the West coast. Those routes paid the most. Not having been back to that area in over 50 years and with the knowledge that the area where Hugh's farm was located has enjoyed tremendous growth, I would not be at all surprised to learn a shopping center was now located where those Appaloosa horses were once grazing.

When it became evident I had no immediate future flying for any airline, we started considering other possibilities like going into business for myself. At the top of our list was a bowling alley for Sedalia. At that time Sedalia did not have one, however bowling nationally had become a very popular sport so logically a new 12- or a 16-lane bowling alley, preferably 16, should have been a very good investment. I talked to the Sedalia city officials, they agreed it was a good idea, and that the city needed one. But sadly, no help was volunteered. I also talked to the Brunswick, Balk, and Collander people in KC who sold bowling alley equipment and as you might guess, they enthusiastically agreed. They even offered to provide limited financial assistance for the alleys and the installation expense. Unfortunately, more help than that was needed. Then I talked to the bankers in Sedalia. They too agreed the idea had merit, but they didn't like the small amount of cash I had to put into it and the fact I was a military man lacking experience in business, so I got a thumbs down on the loan I was seeking to get started. I even approached my dad for some financial backing towards the project but since he had become fully leveraged in buying farmland and knew nothing about bowling, he apologized for having to turn me down, but he couldn't risk losing everything he already had. I understood. He then took me to the local bank to talk to the bank president, perhaps they would grant the necessary loan. The answer was just additional discouragement, and the final blow. They would stick with making farm loans they understood.

The trip to Colorado, the bowling alley fiasco, and all my other dead-end investigations, were completed during the Winter and early Spring of 1947, or before Cheryl was born. Unfortunately, after I was released from the Air Force on Jan 22, our income stopped. Consequently, we were now living off our savings, which obviously could not be sustained, so I started seriously investigating the job market in Kansas City, with the thought that as soon as our first child was born we'd move to KC and start a new life with a new career. The two finalists in my job search came down to a choice between offers I'd received from Hallmark and Sears. Why I chose Sears over Hallmark I don't recall at this time, but I have no regrets. I always liked working at Sears and I always felt they liked me. It would be my only job until I retired.

Cheryl was born on April 7th. Included in my personal file among other things, is a cancelled check dated 4-16-47 in the amount of $69.50 made out to the Bothwell Hospital in Sedalia, Mo. That covered Shirley's hospital expense for her ten-day stay there. I also have a check dated 4-7-47 made out to the Pferffers Flower Shop in Sedalia in the amount of $12.00. I've been unable to find a check in my file made out to a Gynecologist, so maybe I haven't paid him yet, or perhaps I just slipped him some cash. In those days both Hospitals and Doctors charged modest fees. Pardon me for repeatedly reminding you, but prices were incredibly lower in 1947. Today a 10-day stay in any hospital is going to run into several thousand dollars, so if you spent 17% of that amount for flowers, you're going to be delivering a fairly substantial bundle of flowers to somebody. Well, that's what I bought for my wife, and yes Cheryl, both you and your mother were worth it.

I began working at the Sears catalog plant in Kansas City on April 23'rd, or about two weeks after Cheryl was born, earning roughly half of what a Major on flight pay, such as myself, was being paid in the Air Force. Actually, that didn't concern me deeply. I was well aware I was starting at the bottom of an entirely new career, but I was convinced that in time, when I had proved myself, the difference would be more than made up. My beginning pay at Sears was $1.30 per hr. (I still have my original pay envelope and receipt)[31]. That computes out to about $2,704 per year, however I actually made more than that in my first year because Sears honored me with frequent raises. In fact, I was put on checklist (salary) just before the Christmas selling season, which cost me a little at the time, since those on checklist received no extra pay for overtime. In those years the Christmas selling season in the catalog business always involved many overtime hours. At Sears, I started as a trainee in the inspection department but before I had been there a year, I became a rookie buyer in the merchandising organization. Then through the years I worked my way up through the organization as a catalog buyer, Senior Buyer, Merchandise Manager, Group Merchandise Manager, and finally Assistant Merchandise Superintendent.[32]

During that early period I worked at Sears, I also stayed active in the Air Force Reserve. This involved at-

---

[31] Editor's Note: Ironically, that was my starting pay in my first job – as a bus boy when I was 14 in 1968.

[32] Editor's Note: That made him the #2 man at the Dallas Catalog plant, where he transferred in 1979 after they closed the Kansas City plant. By that time, all of us kids were gone from the house. Before then, dad passed up a lot of promotions because they would have involved moving from Kansas City. Neither he nor my mom wanted to do that – mostly for us kids.

tending evening meetings and spending some weekends at a nearby air base. The best part was it also provided some opportunity to do a little flying, which was still in my blood. That part died slow and hard. One weekend I even took John Neff, an operating manager at Sears up for a ride in an A-T6 out of the Fairfax airfield in KC, Kans. He put on his old military uniform, which made riding in a military plane OK. I think he enjoyed the ride, however I also thought he was going to get airsick when the aerobatic maneuvers started, so I quit. He obviously didn t enjoy seeing the world on its side, so I knew better than to give him an upside-down view.

In early 1953 rumors started flying that the 442'nd Troop Carrier Wing that I belonged to at the time was going to be activated and flown to Korea. The 442'nd was equipped with C-46's and was based at the Grandview airfield. This news caused near panic on my part. I'd already started my family, having two children at that time[33], but leaving my wife behind while I went to Korea could have been very damaging to our marriage. Shirley had no immediate family members of her own that she could turn to here in this country for help. It would have been an extremely difficult situation for her had I left. I could even visualize her returning to England with my two daughters while I was overseas. I would have understood, but I wouldn't have liked it, so I moved quickly to see what could be done. Besides I'd already made a good start with Sears and an untimely interruption such as this could damage my career there as well. So I very hastily started checking to see if I had any options. Please, were there any?

---

[33] Editor's Note: My other sister, Juliette, was born November 2, 1949.

Fortunately, there was. I was advised what I should do before it was too late was to fire in a request immediately to be transferred to the inactive, non-affiliated Reserve. That I did, and it was none too soon because I had no sooner received my confirming orders than the 442'nd received their activation orders and were off to Korea leaving me and a few other nervous officers behind. Phew! That was close! That close call sort of cooled me on the Reserves, but yielding to some of my fellow compatriots' suggestions, I requested later that year another transfer, this time to the Standby Reserves. I don't recall what that meant exactly, but I think it entitled me to attend meetings to earn points toward retirement but that's about all. I never did any more flying in the Reserves. In July 1956 I received my promotion to Lt Col. Though I continued attending meetings sporadically until sometime in the early 60's, I finally lost complete interest in the Reserves, and just stopped going. To hell with working to gain points for military retirement pay. My family and my employer needed my time more; besides I was doing well at Sears. I'll build my own retirement nest egg. Besides golf replaced flying as a hobby.

Now, let's go back to when we bought our first house. It was a small three-bedroom, one bath house that we bought using no down payment for the tidy sum of $10,500. Taking advantage of our G. I. loan privilege (for WW2 veterans) we had a 4.5%, 20 yr. loan that left us with monthly loan payments of $63.63, plus monthly payments of $7.70 for taxes and insurance in 1947. By 1955 the taxes and insurance portion had grown to $19.16 per mo. (Lots of new schools had to be built). We lived in our house on El Monte in Prairie Village Kansas until 1955 – a year after my son, John, as born.

Prairie Village was unique. Not for its time, because there were several similar housing developments around the country under construction. Each development, trying to capitalize on the situation was catering to that mass of returning WW2 veterans. Today, a similar development won't be found anywhere. Obviously, the situation is entirely different. Back then a new housing development such as Prairie Village may have had different styles of architecture and different price ranges from its competitors as they do today, but they all had one thing in common. It would be found in its inhabitants. Especially the inhabitants. Since they were all WW2 veterans using government G.I. loans, they were also young. No old folks in their right mind would have ever wanted to buy and live there. Too many kids! Every house contained little kids. Lots of kids -- with more on the way. Our house at its maximum, had three kids and we were below average. Shirley's pet nickname for our street when she wrote home was well put, she called it, "Mothering Heights". By now those kids have grown up, and many are grandparents, but they will always be known as the baby boomers.

In mid-1948, after having lived in our unadorned new residence for about a year, I received a phone call from Jack Martin, an old flying buddy from the 52'nd Fighter Group. He was located somewhere in Southwest Missouri working for the Eagle Pitcher Mining Co. He said he remembered that I was from Protection, Kansas, had called my parents, and was given my present phone number. He said he was leaving on vacation soon and would be traveling through KC and would like to stop by for a short visit to talk a little about our "old 52'nd Fighter Group days" if I was available. I was thrilled to hear from him and insisted that he, his wife Jan, and their little boy spend the night if they could. They could and they did. Not only did they spend the night, they spent several nights, like a week's worth.

In that time Jack told me a lot of things about a lot of pilots. Somehow he had managed to keep up with the whereabouts of just about every former member of the 52'nd and he filled me in on all the interesting and in some cases gory details. It was he, for example, that informed me that Gabriel had crashed into Mt. Ranier. It fascinated me that he knew so much about everyone. He also informed me that after he left our house, he had two more ex-52'nd FG members he planned to visit. Beyond 'our good old flying days' topic, his next most favorite topic of conversation was about his son "Butch", who incidentally was well named. I had no idea a three-year old boy could be so full of energy. It gave me some preview of what to expect from my son, if I ever got one. While the Martin's were there, I took advantage of the occasion to ask Jan what she did with that old Ford Model "B" car that Lt. Smithers and I bought for $50 in Orlando, Fla back in the late Spring of 1942 and left in her custody when we left for overseas. Her answer was that she kept driving it until it finally died permanently sometime during the war.

After they had been there a few days and no definite word had been given as to when they planned to leave, I was beginning to become concerned. So was Shirley. She was taking care of a one-year-old child while cooking, keeping house, and trying to be a gracious hostess. I also began to wonder if perhaps Jack might not be suffering from some form of Post Traumatic Syndrome (PTSD), which was reputed to be fairly common among military survivors. There had been a little about it in the papers but not enough for me to qualify as an expert, so I wasn't too sure how I should react. Nevertheless, after they had been our guests for a full week and had given nothing but evasive, indefinite dates as to when they planned to leave, I finally decided, reluctantly, that it was time for direct positive action. So in the car returning home from the grocery store that evening I told Jack that while we had enjoyed his family's stay very much, it was time for him and Jan to move on. The three Martins loaded up their new Packard and drove off the next morning. I've never heard from him since. Not even a thank you note. I regretted very much having to do what I did, but it was time. As I saw it, I was starting a new life, with a wife, and a baby, and a new occupational career. It was time to let wartime bygones be bygones.

I felt no matter the obstacles, a happy and successful family life was largely dependent upon how willingly one made the sacrifices necessary for a complete conversion from a wartime life to a peacetime family life. Sustaining that transition required a high degree of determination. Shirley and I both had that, particularly Shirley. That's obvious from the results. Shirley devoted full time to the task of mothering her three children and making certain they were safe, healthy, happy, and excelled at school. They did. Furthermore, Shirley never believed in exercising her right to be an employee earning an income for herself and the family. She was more than willing to make that sacrifice and settle for a lower standard of living in exchange for devoting full time to her children and her husband. This was particularly true while the children were young in Elementary through Junior High. She's often said that she considered those first few moments when the kids returned home from school as being some of her most important counseling time of the day. That's when the child unloads all the stressful happenings through the day. According to Shirley's firm belief, as little as a half hour later is too late, by then the child has either forgotten or moved on to new problems. In her way of thinking she was copying the techniques used by many successful winning football and basketball coaches. Often a coach can be seen substituting for a player so the coach can take a particular player aside for a little teaching while it's fresh on both their minds. The coach knows from experience the same corrective teaching that's given when the game is over is not as effective.

Also, while the children were young, Shirley did much more than provide intelligent counseling and guidance. She provided love and constant security. She personally spent her days watching over her brood like a hawk. From the first day after each child was born, she knew exactly where each of her three children were every minute. They were never out of her sight unless they were under someone else's care whom she considered a responsible person. (We found out later, much later, at a few family dinner confession times that when the children reached teenage years, their mother only *thought* she knew exactly where they were). But since all three of our children have master's degrees or better, with one being a medical Doctor. She must have been doing a lot of things right. It's also clear that all three children love their Mother very dearly and fully appreciate every loving thing she's done. Confidentially, I love her very dearly too. Always have!

## Acknowledgements

Information for this book was gathered from a number of sources more reliable than my memory. In particular, many of the pictures seen in this book came from these sources.

Maguire, Jon A. *Gooney Birds & Ferry Tales,* Schiffer Publishing Ltd., Atglen, PA., 1998

Ryan, Cornelius, *The Last Battle*, Simon and Schuster, New York, 1966

**Aviation Enthusiast Corner**, www.aeroweb.org/air.html

**Boeing,** www.boeing.com

**Dan's History,** www.danshistory.com/ww2/vweapon.html

**Ibiblio,**

**Institute for National Strategic Studies**

**University of San Diego,**

**US Air Force Museum,**

**Westmont College,**

www.b25.net/bt13.html/

www.ptsi.net/user/museum/dustbowl.html

*Other titles by BLKDOG Publishing that you may enjoy:*

**Mortal Musings: Waiting for Dawn**
**By John Wait**

**For many of us, cancer is an inescapable reality. It is estimated that one in two people will be affected by the disease during their life. 'Mortal Musings: Waiting for Dawn' is a moving, thought-provoking and intensely personal account of one man's journey.**

In October 2016 my indigestion turned out to be cancer  A few days later, the news got worse when it was discovered my cancer was not only rare and incurable, but it was Stage IV and I likely had only a few months to live. A death sentence like that naturally makes you think about your own mortality and what lies beyond. But I was not about to give in to the inevitable. I refused to believe in a no-win scenario.

People say it is always darkest before the dawn, so I set about waiting for the sunrise. Being impatient, I did everything I could to hurry it along.

Mortal Musings is about my fight -- physically, mentally and spiritually. It is about hope, faith and denial, how the cancer impacted my life and the lives of those around me, my treatments and the emotional struggle I endured. But it also delves into speculation about what lies ahead, beyond this mortal coil. That I am still here, three years later, is a miracle. That I am now cancer free is even more amazing. As Jimmy Valvano said, "don't give up, don't ever give up." And I didn't.

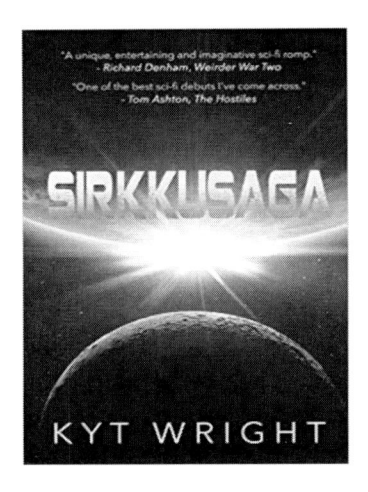

## Sirkkusaga
## By Kyt Wright

*A saga — a long story of heroic achievement, especially a medieval prose narrative in Old Norse or a long, involved story, account, or series of incidents often named for the principal character.*

Several hundred years after a world-shattering war, two of the surviving nations, the Reignweald and the Dominion, have fought themselves to a standstill, both remaining determined to control of what's left of it.

Sirki Vigsdottir, a songstress who performs under the name Freya in folk-rock group *The Harvest*, is a beautiful, self-centered woman who is fond of drink and a recovering addict to boot – not the sort of girl a boy brings home to Mother.

Following an attack from an unexpected quarter, abilities awaken within Sirki, who begins a journey of self-discovery. These new-found skills attract the attention of both the Psi, a mysterious group of telepaths headed by the fearsome Mina and an equally sinister government department – the ACG.

As it becomes clear that her life of self-indulgence is over, Sirki wonders if her new-found powers are a blessing or a curse.

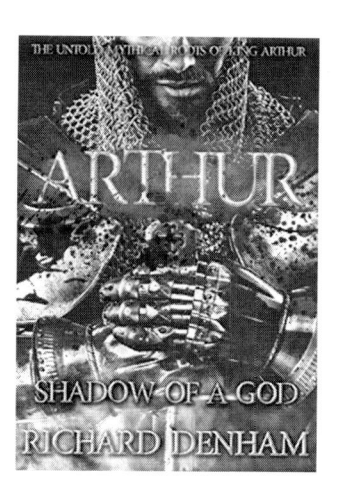

THE UNTOLD MYTHICAL ROOTS OF KING ARTHUR

ARTHUR

SHADOW OF A GOD
RICHARD DENHAM

## Arthur: Shadow of a God
## By Richard Denham

King Arthur has fascinated the Western world for over a thousand years and yet we still know nothing more about him now than we did then. Layer upon layer of heroics and exploits have been piled upon him to the point where history, legend and myth have become hopelessly entangled.

In recent years, there has been a sort of scholarly consensus that 'the once and future king' was clearly some sort of Romano-British warlord, heroically stemming the tide of wave after wave of Saxon invaders after the end of Roman rule. But surprisingly, and no matter how much we enjoy this narrative, there is actually next-to-nothing solid to support this theory except the wishful thinking of understandably bitter contemporaries. The sources and scholarship used to support the 'real Arthur' are as much tentative guesswork and pushing 'evidence' to the extreme to fit in with this version as anything involving magic swords, wizards and dragons. Even Archaeology remains silent. Arthur is, and always has been, the square peg that refuses to fit neatly into the historians round hole.

***Arthur: Shadow of a God*** gives a fascinating overview of Britain's lost hero and casts a light over an often-overlooked and somewhat inconvenient truth; Arthur was almost certainly not a man at all, but a god. He is linked inextricably to the world of

Celtic folklore and Druidic traditions. Whereas tyrants like Nero and Caligula were men who fancied themselves gods; is it not possible that Arthur was a god we have turned into a man? Perhaps then there is a truth here. Arthur, 'The King under the Mountain'; sleeping until his return will never return, after all, because he doesn't need to. Arthur the god never left in the first place and remains as popular today as he ever was. His legend echoes in stories, films and games that are every bit as imaginative and fanciful as that which the minds of talented bards such as Taliesin and Aneirin came up with when the mists of the 'dark ages' still swirled over Britain – and perhaps that is a good thing after all, most at home in the imaginations of children and adults alike – being the Arthur his believers want him to be.

## A Storm of Magic
## By Ashley Laino

Being brought back from the dead is an impressive trick, even for magician Darien Burron. Now he must try and use his sleight of hand to swindle modern-day witch, Mirah, to sign her power away, or end up a tormented demon in the afterlife.

Meanwhile, sixteen-year-old Mirah is starting to lose control of her powers. After an incident at her aunt's Witchery store, Mirah is sent to a secret coven to learn to control her abilities. While away, Mirah meets up with a soft-spoken clairvoyant, a brazen storm witch, and the creator of dark magic itself. The young woman must learn to trust in herself before she loses herself entirely to the darkness that hunts her.

**Weirder War Two**
**By Richard Denham & Michael Jecks**

*Did a Warner Bros. cartoon prophesize the use of the atom bomb? Did the Allies really plan to use stink bombs on the enemy? Why did the Nazis make their own version of Titanic and why were polar bear photographs appearing throughout Europe?*

The Second World War was the bloodiest of all wars. Mass armies of men trudged, flew or rode from battlefields as far away as North Africa to central Europe, from India to Burma, from the Philippines to the borders of Japan. It saw the first aircraft carrier sea battle, and the indiscriminate use of terror against civilian populations in ways not seen since the Thirty Years War. Nuclear and incendiary bombs erased entire cities. V weapons brought new horror from the skies: the V1 with their hideous grumbling engines, the V2 with sudden, unexpected death. People were systematically starved: in Britain food had to be rationed because of the stranglehold of U-Boats, while in Holland the German blockage of food and fuel saw 30,000 die of starvation in the winter of 1944/5. It was a catastrophe for millions.

At a time of such enormous crisis, scientists sought ever more inventive weapons, or devices to help halt the war. Civilians were involved as never before, with women taking up new trades, proving themselves as capable as their male predecessors whether in the factories or the fields.

The stories in this book are of courage, of ingenuity, of hilarity in some cases, or of great sadness, but they are all thought-provoking - and rather weird. So whether you are interested in the last Polish cavalry charge, the Blackout Ripper, Dada, or Ghandi's attempt to stop the bloodshed, welcome to the Weirder War Two!

## Click Bait
## By Gillian Philip

A funny joke's a funny joke. Eddie Doolan doesn't think twice about adapting it to fit a tragic local news story and posting it on social media.

It's less of a joke when his drunken post goes viral It stops being funny altogether when Eddie ends up jobless, friendless and ostracized by the whole town of Langburn. This isn't how he wanted to achieve fame.

Under siege from the press and facing charges not just for the joke but for a history of abusive behavior on the internet, Eddie grows increasingly paranoid and desperate. The only people still speaking to him are Crow, a neglected kid who relies on Eddie for food and company, and Sid, the local gamekeeper's granddaughter. It's Sid who offers Eddie a refuge and an understanding ear.

But she also offers him an illegal shotgun - and as Eddie's life spirals downwards, and his efforts at redemption are thwarted at every turn, the gun starts to look like the answer to all his problems.

## Burning Bridges
## By Chris Bedell

*They've always said that three's a crowd...*

24-year-old Sasha didn't anticipate her identical twin Riley killing herself upon their reconciliation after years of estrangement. But Sasha senses an opportunity and assumes Riley's identity so she can escape her old life.

Playing Riley isn't without complications, though. Riley's had a strained relationship with her wife and stepson so Sasha must do whatever she can to make her newfound family love and accept her. If Sasha's arrangement ends, then she'll have nothing protecting her from her past. However, when one of Sasha's former clients tracks her down, Sasha must choose between her new life and the only person who cared about her.

But things are about to become even more complicated, as a third sister, Katrina, enters the scene...

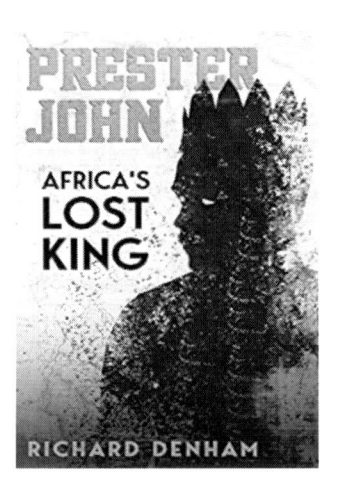

## Prester John
## By Richard Denham

He sits on his jewelled throne on the Horn of Africa in the maps of the sixteenth century. He can see his whole empire reflected in a mirror outside his palace. He carries three crosses into battle and each cross is guarded by one hundred thousand men. He was with St Thomas in the third century when he set up a Christian church in India. He came like a thunderbolt out of the far East eight centuries later, to rescue the crusaders clinging on to Jerusalem. And he was still there when Portuguese explorers went looking for him in the fifteenth century.

He went by different names. The priest who was also a king was Ong Khan; he was Genghis Khan; he was Lebna Dengel. Above all, he was a Christian king who ruled a vast empire full of magical wonders: men with faces in their chests; men with huge, backward-facing feet; rivers and seas made of sand. His lands lay next to the earthly Paradise which had once been the Garden of Eden. He wrote letters to popes and princes. He promised salvation and hope to generations.

But it was noticeable that as men looked outward, exploring more of the natural world; as science replaced superstition and the age of miracles faded, Prester John was always elsewhere. He was beyond the Mountains of the Moon, at the edge of the earth, near the mouth of Hell.

Was he real? Did he ever exist? This book will take you on a journey of a lifetime, to worlds that might have been, but never were. It will take you, if you are brave enough, into the world of Prester John.

www.blkdogpublishing.com

Manufactured by Amazon.ca
Acheson, AB

11675196R00146